"It is wonderful that the voice of a new psy(contemporary cultural, political, and ethi(tween the inner and outer worlds that will future. Cosimo Schinaia is an internationally ιⲥⲥⲟ௚......_ . ing these bridges: here, he explores with impressive effectiveness the difficulties of human beings in developing a realistic, integrated, harmonious, and non-narcissistic vision of their relationship with the world in which they live. His analysis of the problem is broad and accurate, ranging from the 'deeply-micro' of individual subjectivities to the 'extensively-macro' of the mentalities of national and international communities; he also constantly and firmly includes an inter-generational perspective, aimed at the humans of tomorrow. This book is a highly specific, extraordinary contribution of psychoanalysis to the protection of the environment and the human species that lives in it with such frequent self-destructive lack of awareness."

Stefano Bolognini, *past president of the International Psychoanalytical Association*

"A psychiatrist, psychoanalyst, Training Member of the Italian Society of Psychoanalysis, Cosimo Schinaia is also a universal spirit who has published many transdisciplinary books in several languages. In *Psychoanalysis and Ecology*, he challenges the role of psychoanalysis in the urgent fight for the survival of our environment. Through many clinical examples from everyday life as well as from the Almighty economic trends that modify inexorably Earth's landscape and vital balance, he analyzes the unconscious resistances of any human being to acknowledge the magnitude and emergency of the problem. But he also shows how psychoanalysis can help overcome both the denial and anxiety provoked by our present situation, to join forces and stop the disaster and heal our planet."

Florence Guignard, *Training and Supervising Analyst of the Société Psychanalytique de Paris, founder of the European Society for Child and Adolescent Psychoanalysis and founder and past president of the International Psychoanalytical Association's Committee on Child and Adolescent Psychoanalysis*

Psychoanalysis and Ecology

This book presents the psychoanalyst with the question of how our enormously modified environmental conditions determine our subjective mental changes and vice versa.

The gravity of the environmental crisis is amply clear and yet, in the face of such incontrovertible evidence, there is an emotional, more than cognitive, difficulty in comprehending the present reality and its future consequences. In understanding the collective imagination as permeating the individual one and vice versa, this book investigates this relationship of mutual co-determination between the individual traumatic stories told and experienced in the consulting room and the positive or negative environmental attitudes exhibited by patients. The pairing of clinical vignettes with dispatches from the collective imagination sheds light on the confused affective investments and anxieties that propel pathological defenses, such as negation, suppression, intellectualization, displacement, and disavowal. The final chapter concludes with notes on the role of hope in a damaged world and the importance of integrity within the psychoanalytic field and beyond.

This book will be of great interest to psychoanalysts, psychotherapists, and psychiatrists, as well as anthropologists, environmentalists, and ecologists.

Cosimo Schinaia is a training and supervising psychoanalyst of the SPI and a full member of the IPA, working in private practice in Genoa, Italy. He is the author of several books, including *On Paedophilia* (2010) and *Psychoanalysis and Architecture* (2016), translated in several languages. *Psychoanalysis and Ecology* is also available in Italian, French, and Spanish.

Psychoanalysis and Ecology
The Unconscious and the Environment

Cosimo Schinaia

Routledge
Taylor & Francis Group

LONDON AND NEW YORK

Cover Image: Gwengoat / Getty Images

First published in English 2022
by Routledge
4 Park Square, Milton Park, Abingdon, Oxon OX14 4RN

and by Routledge
605 Third Avenue, New York, NY 10158

Routledge is an imprint of the Taylor & Francis Group, an informa business

Published in Italian by Alpes Italia, Rome 2020

British Library Cataloguing-in-Publication Data
A catalogue record for this book is available from the British Library

Library of Congress Cataloging-in-Publication Data
Names: Schinaia, Cosimo, 1951- author.
Title: Psychoanalysis and ecology: the unconscious and the
environment / Cosimo Schinaia.
Other titles: Inconscio e l'ambiente. English
Description: Abingdon, Oxon; New York, NY: Routledge, 2022. |
Includes bibliographical references. |
Identifiers: LCCN 2021045535 (print) | LCCN 2021045536 (ebook) |
ISBN 9781032114828 (paperback) | ISBN 9781032114798 (hardback) |
ISBN 9781003220077 (ebook)
Subjects: LCSH: Ecology—Psychological aspects. |
Subconsciousness. | Environmental psychology. | Psychoanalysis.
Classification: LCC BF353.5.N37 S3513 2022 (print) |
LCC BF353.5.N37 (ebook) | DDC 155.9/1—dc23
LC record available at https://lccn.loc.gov/2021045535
LC ebook record available at https://lccn.loc.gov/2021045536

ISBN: 978-1-032-11479-8 (hbk)
ISBN: 978-1-032-11482-8 (pbk)
ISBN: 978-1-003-22007-7 (ebk)

DOI: 10.4324/9781003220077

Typeset in Times New Roman
by codeMantra

To Margherita

Contents

Acknowledgments

I want to thank Sally Weintrobe for her foreword to this edition. It is both an honor and pleasure. In fact, her foreword demonstrates her long and passionate involvement in studying the individual and collective resistances that prevent the awareness that the issues related to climate change and, in general, to the environmental crisis are of the utmost urgency.

I am grateful to Lorena Preta, coordinator of the group of *Geography of Psychoanalysis* of the International Psychoanalytical Association. I appreciated very much her passionate foreword to the Italian edition of the book, from which emerges her psychoanalytic culture, on the one hand, deeply entrenched in tradition, and on the other, open to new psychosocial realities.

I am also grateful to Luca Mercalli, President of the Italian Meteorological Society, whose contributions here greatly enrich my work with thought-provoking suggestions and well-considered commentary. Luca offered his peculiar expertise through the point of view of a curious and smart environmentalist, which he is.

I am grateful to Stefano Bolognini and Florence Guignard for their endorsements, which show their love for Nature and their psychoanalytic knowledge.

Riccardo Brunacci, Jean-Pierre D'Haenens, Marie Antoinette Ferroni, Mireille Fognini, Alfredo Lombardozzi, Dimitris Malidelis, Giacomo Orlando, Mario Pennuzzi, Enrico Pinna, and Jacopo Schinaia kindly read the book at different stages. Thus, they helped along its evolution and provided relevant comments and suggestions. I am very grateful to them for their patience.

I am also grateful to Joseph Dodds, Renee Lertzman, Luc Magnenat, and Sally Weintrobe. Their books, so rich in important contributions from varied areas of thinking, put environmental topics at the center of the international psychoanalytic debate. They inspired me tremendously.

I cannot forget to thank to Giuseppe Lo Dico and Kathryn Haralambous for their, not only expert and clear but also emotionally involved, English translation of the book.

Foreword to the English edition

Sally Weintrobe[1]
I am so pleased to be asked to write this foreword to the English edition of Cosimo Schinaia's book on the ecological crisis. Henry James described death as "the distinguished thing," thus emphasizing its gravitas. In my view, the ecological crisis is today's "distinguished thing." It is *the* issue of our time and it involves death on a large scale. Indeed, some commentators are now calling our era the beginning of the Necrocene. The temptation is to disavow the gravitas with strategies, such as "minimization," "normalization," or "disappearing." Schinaia's warm, engaging, and intimate style helps us to stay with the subject.

This book is erudite. In highlighting that I want to thank Schinaia, in particular, for drawing together and summarizing so much of the work on climate and ecology undertaken by human scientists, most of it in the past decade. Scientists are leaving their academic silos and connecting to collectively study which circumstances lead people to be more likely to disavow reality and – crucially – which psychic, social, and material conditions are needed to ensure that life is sustainable. Cosimo brings in ideas from psychoanalysis, analytical psychology, group psychology, ecopsychology, ethics, philosophy, social psychology, anthropology, literature, sociology, psychosocial studies, complexity theory, geography, architecture, and town planning. I picture this collaborative enterprise as birds of a feather taking off, empowered by what I call "the new imagination." As Cosimo's analysis makes clear, this imagination seeks interdisciplinarity and it is open to being influenced by what it finds. It is curious, not conquering, and it seeks to connect.

Cosimo mounts a cogent critique of the concept of "applied" (as opposed to "pure" individual clinical) psychoanalysis. His point is that defenses operate at different levels: within the individual, in groups, and at the general level of the human. Defenses bear a strong family resemblance across these scales, making them as recognizable as fractal patterns that repeat. His critique is not of the psychoanalytic theory itself, but of a still widespread way in which it is framed. Indeed, Freud had viewed psychoanalysis as a general theory of mind, with clinical work being only one of its applications.

Particular ways of "applying" theory are being challenged across disciplines. Here are two examples from architecture and economics. Sue Roaf, Professor of Urban Design (2018), described what she called a "20th Century architecture" that starts with a preformed conception of a building and then builds it without regard for context or locale. "Think Dubai," she said. She called for a 21st century architecture that engages with the wider ecology and is open to influence by that ecology. An example is, do we maintain a technologically controlled even temperature inside a standard building, or do we design buildings in ways that work with weather patterns and how peoples' bodies adjust to them? This question can also serve as a metaphor: do we screen off climate reality and remain in a bubble of disavowal in which conflict and anxiety are minimized, or are we open to reality and to being modified by it?

The dominant economic frame at present is founded on an imperative of endless growth. Again, this thinking is divorced from any consideration of environmental limits. In *Beyond the Limits*, the complexity theorist Donella Meadows (1972) exposed and confounded "endless growth" framing with a simple diagram of a square *inside* a circle. The square was economics and the circle represented the wider ecology. Both Roaf and Meadows were signaling the need for "bounded" theory, theory embedded within a specific context. They were both challenging the idea that models and theoretical systems can be "applied." Indeed, psychoanalytic "application" of this kind has led to justified criticism for it being ahistorical.

"Applied" thinking can run the risk of being closed thinking, less open to learning from and being changed by experience. We are witnessing a paradigm shift in the human and the natural sciences as both branches break with and transcend this kind of closed thinking that I suggest is symptomatic of a modernity that insists nature is there to be managed and conquered, and nature must "fit in." The shift is to a mindset that recognizes it is we who fit in with, are formed by and find our limits within, a wider ecology.

Cosimo outlines in detail Freud's writings on the environment and reminds us how seminal Robert Searles' pioneering work would prove for those who came later. In 1972, Searles accurately diagnosed the problem humanity faces when he presciently said, "In the pull upon us to become omnipotently free of human conflict, we are in danger of bringing about our extinction." Conflict is only truly faced when it is appreciated that there are limits to desire, greed, and entitlement.

The neoliberal era – roughly the past 40 odd years – has seen Exceptionalism soar (see Weintrobe, 2021). Exceptionalism in politics and in general culture involves feeling entitled to use omnipotent thinking to self-idealize, to justify ignoring limits and boundaries, and to make the conflicts that are generated, especially moral conflict "disappear". Omnipotent thinking reduces in "as if" ways any felt conflict about greed, generating waste, and squandering, subjects that Cosimo explores in depth. I particularly valued the way he shows, with clinical material, what psychoanalysis can offer to an understanding of humanity's failure to live within its means.

As Leopold Aldo famously said, to have an environmental education is to live in a world of wounds. As we read this book, we become aware that we are not conquerors of nature but walking wounded in her defiled presence. Here Cosimo helps us by introducing a personal note, talking of his grief at finding the world of his childhood so transformed and degraded. We now have so much to mourn as we confront damage and loss outside and inside us.

I was particularly interested in his section on work, in which he exposes the facile argument – the false binary – that says to workers in a particular locale, "You can have either jobs or a beautiful environment that is sustainable, but not both. You choose." Cosimo debunks this argument. I would add that this uncaring framing carries the potential implication that it is workers who are meant to bear the guilt of damage that is actually mainly caused by a manufacturing class that pursues only profit and disrespects people and planet. People are entitled to work and to an environment that feeds the spirit.

The chapters in this book build a case that enables the power of an analytic approach to shine through. His detailed *historically specific* analyses reveal clinical facts (defenses, evidence of trauma, and traumatic wounds) at the level of the individual and the group. By delving into patients' material, he shows the complex ways in which trauma, both individual and collective, can thread itself into and onto social issues. It made me look at the word "material" in a new light. As psychoanalysts, we are very familiar with the idea of clinical material. All too often, we treat this "material" in reductive ways as "standing for" human objects relations (again ablating the wider context and environment, or treating it as *only* metaphor). In Cosimo's account, it is clear that "material" is the stuff that the mind, including the unconscious mind, gets to work on. A psychic construction is made from intertwined inner subjective elements and from material elements in the external world: the water we squander, the degraded landscapes we mourn. The human mind treats all this as "material" that it struggles to sift and locate as belonging inside or outside us or both.

Foreword to the Italian edition

Lorena Preta[2]

Perhaps a new area has begun for psychoanalysis, one characterized by the deep intuitions of Freudian and post-Freudian psychoanalysis, but free from the worries of being stigmatized as intuitions of the so-called applied psychoanalysis or of an unqualified and inefficacious theory if extended beyond its boundaries. Further, this new era does not consider psychoanalytic thought to be a product of a "high-level" doctrine that cannot be contaminated by what is real. This allows psychoanalysis to find the deep meaning of its own peculiarity, something Freud had in mind from the beginning.

Psychoanalysis can help us comprehend individual and collective facts without hiding their problematic aspects, but rather by exalting them as unavoidable objects of inquiry.

It is an era of assessing the complexity of and the various levels that define reality. We cannot ignore this reality at the cost of impoverishing our thought and detaching from the practice of life. Today, the practice of life presents itself as a dangerous process, full of ambiguities and risks, lively, quick, sometimes painful, something that prevents us from ceasing to think and act.

This book by Cosimo Schinaia pushes us on that most urgent topic – the environment. It tackles the environmental crisis through various quotations and references, refined but very close to the reality we deal with every day, the reality that affects every one of us.

I do not intend to reconsider here the clearly defined and described stages of psychoanalysis and the other disciplines the book discusses. Rather, I intend to write about what I felt when I thought about this foreword. This is because I believe it clearly represents the position that the author implicitly invites us to take about the ecological problem.

In general, when one writes or considers a certain topic, one must remove oneself and examine personal references, read up on the subject, perhaps update one's opinions on it. But, when I reflected on this book, I found it impossible to disconnect myself.

I believe it is compulsory to pay attention to what Schinaia writes and argues, to make a clear, neat, and defined choice about environmental crises. When you read this book, you soon recognize that these problems cannot be avoided in any way.

I deem this book necessary. We cannot move away from its message, take our time, or hesitate. We must face the brutality of things that reality puts in front of us – reality as it is, without any rhetorical devices or arbitrary dismissals.

With a fluid writing style, Schinaia invites the reader to reconstruct and enlarge his reference map regarding the environment.

Inside–outside, individual–group, nature–culture are some of the dichotomies Schinaia provides as landmarks for this ecological journey. With these dichotomies, he connects the reader to basic reality. Every term is meaningful only if it is connected to its opposite: it is their interdependence that constitutes the complexity of things. To not consider one of the terms or the interrelationship between the two would be tantamount to a sort of amputation, a limitation.

In fact, it is impossible to write about individual imagination without considering the collective imagination that is rooted at its basis. They are in a relationship of mutual co-determination.

Nor can we consider an image of an environment only as an external world, not dependent on the representation we have of it in our internal world. For example, it would be impossible to build a house, a home, or one of the objects we produce, without thinking that it does not depend, at least in part, on the projection of some conscious or unconscious parts of our mind.

So, too, it is impossible to consider the age-old controversial dichotomy between nature and culture without keeping in mind that this dichotomy is uninteresting if it does not consider a bidirectional relationship. Such a relationship must be conceived not in terms of opposition but rather in terms of co-construction. The book treats these topics from many different perspectives.

But what Gregory Bateson defines "the pattern that connects" through an epistemological link between nature and culture, that Cosimo Schinaia quotes and exalts, is not always evident. Too often we consider various environmental challenges as being disconnected from one another. Or we strongly deny any possibility for a collective solution.

More than any other theory and practice, psychoanalysis is entrusted with the task of comprehending why, in the face of so much evidence of such serious and dangerous damage to the environment, humankind is almost unable to understand what has happened and what could still happen.

As the book brilliantly points out, there is a multitude of defense mechanisms, such as splitting, intellectualization, negation, repression, suppression, displacement, and disavowal. Each offers a solution that masks the anxiety emanating from awareness of the danger, rendering it impossible to repair the material, psychological, and moral damage. I want to stress that with the adjective "moral" I refer to the ethical dimension of our mind, that specific dimension that makes it human.

Sometimes it seems as if the awareness of the danger should come from the outside, perhaps from an extraterrestrial civilization, as in the classic science-fiction film *The Day the Earth Stood Still* (1951) by Robert Wise, in which extraterrestrials want to make humankind aware of its destructiveness and try to correct it.

It is we who impede our own awareness of the danger and the damage made to the biosphere. It is our internal world, our multitude of conscious and unconscious ways that make it impossible for us to open our eyes to reality.

The anxiety that can destroy the individual is what blinds us to this awareness and, as Schinaia clearly argues, it is not only an individual but also a collective defense mechanism. In Schinaia's words, it is crucial for us to integrate "the anxious feelings of loss" and finitude to "find an authentic relationship with a dynamic and uncertain world."

It is also crucial that we avoid the opposite reaction, that is, the uncritical exaltation of the natural world that leads to "a conformist and fanatic adhesion to ecologist ideology," a sort of group hallucination.

The book considers many topics. The points of view intersect, often are in opposition, to provide an explanation that considers the innumerable aspects of the problem.

Throughout the book, we find clinical vignettes that define characters and vicissitudes, showing how our mind and experience can be affected by mental obstructions leading to complex behaviors. Examples of these behaviors include wasting water and resources or obsessively seeking protection from external agents that are experienced as contaminative. These behaviors reflect a complex twist of the personal and collective dimension. They make clear that psychoanalysis, better than other disciplines, allows us to comprehend how personal experiences and internal dynamics can reflect the problematic relations with the environment.

I found the author's personal reference to a painful event in Italian history, regarding ILVA, an Italian steelwork company based in Taranto very thought-provoking. The pollution produced by the company over many years had many fatal consequences that are yet to be resolved. Schinaia comes from Taranto. Through his memories of a past that no longer exists and that can only be part of his personal narrative, he not only explains to his reader the deleterious effects of the contamination and the poisoning of the water, soil, and air, but he also outlines how this situation relates to labor and employment matters. In Taranto, people must face the paradox of

ILVA saving them from poverty and, simultaneously, condemning them to killing nature and their fellow beings.

In science fiction novels and films, extraterrestrials are sometimes aggressive conquerors (very similar to us), but sometimes they are attentive intergalactic observers who realize that our planet is beautiful and extraordinary, full of water, vegetation, and many forms of life.

In *The Day the Earth Stood Still*, there is an extraterrestrial phrase ("*Klaatu, Barada, Nikto!*") to prevent any retaliation against aggressive and obtuse humans. In the film, this phrase works very well. But what about us, as we struggle to find a translation system to facilitate communication among various people from several countries in the external world and to bind the varied and numerous levels of our mental organization? Will we be able to find a similar phrase to halt our attacks on the survival of humankind?

Perhaps we do know this phrase, but we do not realize that we should say it to ourselves.

Notes

1 Fellow, British Psychoanalytical Society, and Chair, International Psychoanalytic Association Climate Committee, she is editor of *Engaging with the Climate Change: Psychoanalysis and Interdisciplinary Perspective*, Routledge: Abington and New York, 2013. Her last book in press is *Psychological Roots of the Climate Crisis: Neoliberal Exceptionalism and the Culture of Uncare*, Bloomsbury: New York and London. March 2021.
2 Full Member of Italian Psychoanalytic Society and Chair of International Psychoanalytical Association's Geographies of Psychoanalysis group.

Introduction – the role of psychoanalysis

This book was thought and mostly written before the global pandemic that has been seriously, unexpectedly, and deeply changing the human condition. The lack of attention to the loss of biodiversity in ecosystems has favored the onset of the COVID-19 pandemic. The overexploitation of soil and related changes in its use and the destruction of wildlife have increased the risk of infectious diseases. This has occurred because humans and pets have become closer to pathogen-carrying wildlife. Thus, ecological processes controlling diseases have been disrupted or destroyed. Today, because the conflict between our individual freedoms, guaranteed by the principle of self-determination and the needs of social protection, guaranteed by the principle of collective utility, is so acute, it is highly necessary to explore the link between individual suffering, symbolic organizations, and healing and caring practices of our community. This can be done through the osmosis between inside and outside spheres, consciousness and unconsciousness, mental organization and social organization, nature and culture, the bustle between "in" and "out," mental space and external space, the instable and continuous redefinition of these two areas through their changes, transformations, and reorganizations. These are all thorny issues in a double register, intrapsychic and interpersonal (Schinaia, 2014).

The environment surrounds us. We breathe it and depend on it. At the same time, the environment dwells inside of us, in our minds, dreams, conflicts, anguishes, and fears.

In *Phrases* (1886), Arthur Rimbaud writes that he stretched ropes from steeple to steeple; garlands from window to window; golden chains from star to star, and he dances.

Jean-Bertrand Pontalis (1986) argues that we need many places inside of us to hope to be ourselves.

In the most recent Italian edition of my book *Interno Esterno* (Schinaia, 2016, p. XXIV), I note that the word "text" (from the Latin "*textus*") means texture. I hope that my reader will be able to recognize the *fil rouge* of this text and benefit from my personal considerations on an extremely composite but rich and lively framework of theories, observations, points of view, and

DOI: 10.4324/9781003220077-1

reflections. I hope he can gain access to bliss by the cohabitation of languages working side by side (Barthes, 1973).

To foster exchanges between the inside and the outside, it is necessary to build containers, places of transition, and interconnection.

The conversation among different scientific and cultural languages produces models connecting different and disconnected areas of knowledge and allows for the structure of various and original forms of language and experience. These forms cannot be the sum of the original languages and experiences but something emerging from them, with their own configuration, and an autonomous and original life.

I intend to show how psychoanalysis must not be considered as a luxury good but rather as a crucial source that can help define the individual and group defense mechanisms that obstruct our awareness of today's grave ecological problems – the catastrophes and the challenges we must face. Although I leave all questions on the table, I stress the relevance of an ongoing discussion with other forms of knowledge, expertise, and language. This can be accomplished without any pretentious conquering ambitions or, at the other end of the spectrum, without any search for a totalizing harmony. What makes this discussion possible is the certainty of the importance of psychoanalytic culture and experience that can offer resources, tools, and processes to constructively face our ecological challenges.

I stress that this is not a revival of the old concept of applied psychoanalysis, that is, a subjective, ahistorical, basically reductionistic, and pathologizing explanation and interpretation of an interpreter of external reality, an interpreter who does not accept the possibility of a confirmation or a falsification from such a reality, and who reduces everything to the unconscious working and its decryption without considering the richness of its meanings.

In his VII Seminar (1959–1960) on *The Ethics of Psychoanalysis*, Jacques Lacan proposes an "involved psychoanalysis," a psychoanalysis that, in spite of its enormous and well-defined body of work, is still able to enrich itself, thanks to theoretical and clinical terms derived from other cultures. Thus, psychoanalysis can become a living, evolving organism that is able to understand and imagine which humanity is taking form or, rather, which humanity we are constructing (Preta, 2019a).

Luc Magnenat (2019a) says that psychoanalysis should not be *applied* but *interested* (from the Latin "*inter esse*," to be within).

The question is, how do we face the strong contradiction between the images of progress, the unstoppable, and unlimited development, something that was erected as an unattainable model, on the one hand, and, on the other, the famines and the disturbing information about climate to which we are exposed on a daily basis?

What happens to our sentimental neurons, to our small emotional wills, that, in spite of existential alarms, continue to love, dream, and think about an escape or how to survive (Neri, 2020)?

Our relationship with the climate crisis is characterized by up and down, crazy moments and passions. The environmental risk is a sort of doppel-gänger we must face (Offil, 2020).

How full of contradictions is the human condition! We exterminate other species and then we struggle to save them from extinction; we destroy the ecosystem and then we mobilize to save the planet; we build frail buildings and, after an earthquake, we discover our heroic virtues, we risk our lives to extricate even one soul from the ruins (De Renzis, 2020).

Climate change is a sensitive and controversial subject that generates a hot and polemical debate, characterized not only by preoccupations and questions but also by suspicions and indifference. The environment has become an inseparable symbol of modern society (Berger and Roques, 2016).

Today we tend to study only what we can measure. As a result, we exclude areas of human subjectivity such as our feelings toward nature, climate change, and our empathy and connection with other species (Weintrobe, 2013a).

In his comment to the testimony of Saint Francis of Assisi, Pope Francis (2015) notes that an integral ecology calls for openness to categories that transcend the language of mathematics and biology, and take us to the heart of what it is to be human.

Pope Francis' epistemic attitude finds support in the words that Albert Einstein seems to have written on the blackboard of his office at the Institute for Advanced Studies in Princeton, New Jersey (USA)[1]: *"Not everything that counts can be counted, and not everything that can be counted counts."* Einstein's quote is significant because it stresses the role that emotional subjective features play in the context of natural sciences.

The words of Pope Francis and Albert Einstein should be seriously considered in the many environmental discussions that are based only on the descriptive and dramatically objective side of the catastrophe we face and that do not consider the strength of mental defenses at the individual and group level. These defenses weaken our awareness of the damage we both created and suffer.

Vittorio Lanternari (2003) coined the term *eco-anthropocentrism* to define that conceptual and experiential space in which the *ecological* and the *anthropological* properly articulate themselves. This is the place *par excellence* in which human and non-human factors are in connection among them in multiple ways, in both resonance and conflict, and from which can come fractures and possible future repairs (Lombardozzi, 2006).

Philippe Descola (2005) starts from his fieldwork on the Jivaros Achuar tribes of the Amazon for stating that it is necessary to go beyond the distinction between nature and culture that the Western world considers fundamental. Actually, this distinction is not very explanatory because it postulates, on the one hand, an "objective" world, something of a hard, stable, and an autonomous nature and, on the other, the world of contingencies, that is, of culture or cultures. He proposes a new theoretical approach allowing the continuity/discontinuity distribution between the human being and its environment. Animals, plants, minerals, water, and mountains are not simply that nature to exploit or protect, but parts of a collectivity we and the other creatures belong to in the same manner and with the same rights.

In light of the analysis of the political, scientific, technological, and economic aspects of global warming, science, technology, and economics cannot deliver and maintain satisfying results by themselves, but we must put the ethical dimension of the problem at the center of the international debate (Rich, 2019).

The ethical dimension is a praxis oriented toward the creation of a paradigm of a happiness and desire for something alternative that what we already know, a paradigm free from the contemporary capitalistic system, which prescribes a model of limitless progress and profit maximization that orients individual and collective choices to aggressively exploit environmental resources (Benasayag, 2020).

Rabbi Jonathan Sacks (2020) stresses that the good of a single individual cannot overlook all the community, the moral interconnection with others. Without this interconnection, we risk decadence, social destabilization, the reduction of freedom, dignity, and solidarity. He proposes a "cultural climate change" in opposition to the contradiction between the current degree of wealth (certainly increased throughout the world) and the lack of individual happiness. Sacks' proposal aims also to contrast the role of social media in the modification of the nature of interpersonal relationships, in particular, when they put at the center of life the Self, self-esteem, individualism, self-realization, and self-expression, rather than society.

Globalized society and the contemporary historical-cultural context strongly influence all subjectivities, both at the individual and societal levels.

The historian Aldo Schiavone (2020) argues that this is the greatest change in human history: we are near the frontier dividing two worlds, the natural and the cultural. This is because it has become difficult to distinguish between what is naturally created and what is technically and culturally produced.

The great speed of climate change brings suffering to all human beings and puts into question the foundations of our thought, choices, and certainties (Magnason, 2019).

Lorena Preta (2018) beseeches us to face our mental changes determined by the changing environmental conditions. For her, psychoanalysis is a well-structured discipline, at least as a therapeutic method, which prescribes a direct and exclusive meeting with the patient's internal world, with his phantasmatic and driving forces, and that aims to construct a peculiar analytic space in which the analyst's and the patient's unconscious can confront them. In spite of the focus on internal dynamics, psychoanalysis cannot avoid dealing with enormous environmental changes and with how they can modify the point of view about the mental realm and its dynamics.

Psychoanalysis must deeply inquire on the new geometries of the mind, the new discontents of civilization, the new declinations of the mental sufferance related to the crumbling traditional identity structures and the metapsychic guarantors as we used to know them.

Jacques Press (2019) stresses the many difficulties inherent in facing a new and critical reality, in looking for new anchor points when we are disorientated in the difficult time between the "no longer" and the "not yet." He asks how it is possible to think when our house is on fire. There is a gap between the need for urgent action related to a crisis, on the one hand, and the collapse of our mental functioning, on the other, particularly because we are the agents of destruction. He argues that there is a serious risk of concrete theorizing, of embracing psychoanalytic concepts in an uncritical manner in a highly complex situation that requires new ways of thinking.

Bion (1990) argues that we are in such an advanced stage to understand how big our problems are, but not so much to know how to solve them.

To face a new reality, we must use both new and old tools and go beyond what we have known. Thus, he suggests that the analyst's role is to imagine what another person has experienced. Thus, the analyst's role is to imagine, otherwise we are lost: not imagining is to deny what actually occurred. This demands that we use imagination even when what appears in front of us looks like a hole, a blank image, a vacuum without a cavity. More radically, this means we must imagine what has disappeared and been taken apart, the deleted traces and clues (Fédida et al., 2007).

We must risk new analyses, create new mental tools, propose new modes of comprehension, allowing to consider again and provisionally the relationship with the stranger we chose as our way of being in the world (Kaës, 2013).

Today psychoanalysts must, on the one hand, refer to a psychoanalysis culture strongly rooted in the tradition and, on the other, must have their minds so open to face the new psychosocial realities and deeply understand the new discontents of civilization, the novel forms of psychical suffering related to the disintegration of the traditional structures of identity, of the metapsychic guarantors as we knew them until now.

Chapter 1 assesses the current environmental crisis, its peculiarities and consequences, the attempts to solve it, and the collaborative agreements but also the disagreements that delay a solution.

Chapter 2 proposes a strong interrelation among all living beings and all species as an antidote to the destruction of the ecosystem. The main focus of the chapter is the need to develop a concept of urban planning that balances construction and green space and which has at its core the repair of the city. The chapter concludes with the topic of transgenerational transmission and the legacy we will leave our children.

Chapter 3 is divided in two parts: the first part describes Freud's romantic relationship with nature, based on his own letters from the mountains and the sea and some preparatory notes to *"Civilization and Its Discontents"* (1930); the second assesses Freud's contradictory thoughts about the relationship between humans and nature, because they explicitly express his ideas about the environment and its relevance about the progress and development of our civilization.

Chapter 4 focuses on the development of post-Freud psychoanalytic theory about nature and the environment, and stresses a significant difficulty of psychoanalysts in confronting ecological topics. Only in the 1960s did Harold Searles start to deal with these issues, paving the way for a reflection that would be reconsidered in the 2000s, when the issues of pollution and global warming became urgent. This marked the beginning of an inquiry on those pathological defenses at both the individual and group level that prevent a full and mature awareness of the gravity of the situation.

Chapter 5 addresses the diverse symbolic meanings of waste. Clinical vignettes illustrate how different neurotic aspects of personality and different personal histories play a crucial role in the relationship between human beings and refuse, sometimes resulting in inadequate, incoherent, and risky attitudes and behaviors.

Chapter 6 delves into wasted resources in the home, such as water and heat, and, more generally, consumerism, by interweaving clinical stories and the interdependence between the internal world and the environment.

Chapter 7 discusses how the psychophysical well-being of human beings and other species is under attack by ambient disturbances. Pollution and the attitude toward dark and light, on the one hand, and sounds and silence, on the other hand, emanate from individual histories and conflicts and can be worked through in the therapeutic relationship.

Chapter 8 outlines the connection, similarities, and differences between individual and group defense mechanisms. The chapter assesses defensive features typical of certain militant environmentalists that can reduce the impact of their message. Examples include fanatic adherence to environmentalism, acritical exaltation of the natural world, obsessive dramatization of environmental defense practices and opposition to scientific progress. These defense mechanisms idealize the relationship between man and nature to the point of distorting it, misrepresenting it, and rendering it rhetorical and basically unauthentic. Further, proposing only quick and practical actions for climate change is generally terroristic or, at best, blaming and destined to fail because they do not consider people's confused affective investments, memories, desires, and anxieties.

Chapter 9 examines the painful contradiction between psychophysical well-being (and thus healthy environments) and the right to work. It ventures on a historical–sentimental journey between Taranto, where I was born, and Genoa, where I live, two Italian cities in which steel plants have wrought dire consequences in terms of livability and environmental sustainability.

Finally, Chapter 10 takes stock of the reflections and the arguments of the previous chapters. It proposes possible ideas to adopt to avoid the nostalgia–utopia mindset and suggests realistic and optimistic means of dealing with the environmental crisis at both the individual and group level.

Note

1 At least, as W. B. Cameron reports in his 1963 book.

Chapter 1

Main steps to mitigate the climate emergency

Unanimously approved by the United Nations General Assembly on December 6, 1988, the "Protection of Global Climate for Present and Future Generations of Humankind" formed the basis for the process that led to the 1992 Framework Convention on Climate Change, the 1997 Kyoto Protocol (ratified by 192 countries), and the 2009 Copenhagen Accord. Large countries with a developing economy and an abundance of natural and strategic resources, such as China and India, asked for more time to adhere to the latter and did not agree to being placed on the same level as the large Western nations, which had enjoyed industrialization unfettered by rules guarding against environmental damage.

Approved by 196 countries at the 2015 United Nations Climate Change Conference in Paris, the resolution starts with a basic claim: "Climate change represents an urgent and potentially irreversible threat to human societies and the planet."

The agreement requires maximum cooperation to reduce greenhouse gas emissions. It states that it would enter into force in 2020 only if 55 countries that produce at least 55% of the world's greenhouse gas emissions ratify, accept, and approve it.

The agreement contemplates:

– Keeping the global temperature well below 2°C. About 200 countries aimed to limit the temperature increase above pre-industrial levels and thus even further to 1.5°C, per the Copenhagen Accord. To reach this goal, the countries had to begin to reduce the emissions by 2020.
– A global agreement. In contrast to what happened about six years ago, when an agreement was not reached, all committed to limit emissions, even the biggest polluters, such as China, Europe, India, and the United States.
– Five-year term controls. The objectives must be reviewed every five years. In 2018, the countries were asked to limit emissions to be ready for 2020. Thus, the first review is to occur in 2023.

DOI: 10.4324/9781003220077-2

- Funding for sustainable and renewable energy. Starting in 2020, the more advanced industrialized countries would dedicate a minimum of 100 billion USD per year to promote green technologies and limit carbon use throughout the world. The new financial aim is to be achieved more or less by 2025, toward which investment management firms could contribute.
- Refunding for the neediest countries. The agreement establishes a mechanism for compensating the financial losses created by climate change in the most geographically vulnerable (and often poorest) countries.
- Climate equity. Rich countries must reduce to zero their emissions in the next 12 years so that poor countries can improve living conditions by building infrastructures, hospitals, water supply, and electricity networks.

During the G20 Hangzhou summit in 2016, the mayors of the world's most important cities asked national leaders to band together against the global threat of climate change and to build a world based on low-emission economy and climate security. The presidents of China and the United States and later the European Community announced their formal adhesion to the Paris Agreement. This indicated that more than 55 countries would have agreed to the agreement by 2020, as was predicted in 2015. It is worth noting that in 2015, as in 2014, the world economy grew without registering an increase of global CO_2[1] emissions. Nonetheless, the World Meteorological Organization reported that the CO_2 in the atmosphere crossed the "psychological threshold" of 400 parts per million. This means that the quantity of CO_2 produced in the past years had started to decrease but not so much as to be reabsorbed by so-called carbon sinks such as oceans and big forests. Reaching atmospheric concentration levels of about 450 parts per million (ppm) of CO_2 means an increase of 2.1°C. Thus, levels 350 parts per million CO_2 eq means an increase of temperature of 1°C. To avoid difficulties in managing climate change, the CO_2 levels in the atmosphere must be stabilized by 2030.

In 2017, the Trump Administration threw into question the adhesion to the Paris Agreement by canceling the Clean Power Plan of the Obama Administration, which planned restrictions of industrial emissions, reductions of coal-fired power plants, and a refusal to sign a joint declaration on climate at the 2017 G7 Rome Energy Ministerial Meeting.[2]

Regarding Donald Trump's position, Paul Hoggett (2013) argues that, in the first phases of any scientific inquiry, skepticism can play an important role in developing a solid body of evidence. But once evidence is established, then the skeptical position can become an obstinate persistence in what is untrue or unreasonable skepticism can become a perversion. In the climate change debate, this perversion is evident when skeptics argue that science provides only estimates, not proof. Skeptics demand absolute truth and annihilate the truth-value of accumulated evidence and theory because of its absence.

Skepticism perversely leads, first, to simplifying the problem, second, to adopting reductionist relativism, and, third, to denying climate change. The truth is reversed and well-confirmed scientific data and discoveries are deemed as unproven and, at best, as mere conjectures. One of the main theses supporting climate change denial is the idea that there are regular and cyclic oscillations in temperature trends. It is true that there are climate changes that do not depend on human intervention, but it is also true that they occur very slowly. The historian Emmanuel Le Roy Ladurie (1967) calls supporters of these theses (always falsified by the evidence) as possessed by the demon of "cyclo-mania."

However, Europe, China, and other main world economies adhere to the Paris Agreement, promote the use of renewable energy, and recognize the merits of the so-called "green economy" (Jamieson and Mancuso, 2017). At the same time, Brazilian President Jair Bolsonaro recently promoted dangerous new deforestation projects in the Amazon by advancing the typical arguments of climate change deniers.

The 2018 United Nations Climate Change Conference in Katowice marked an important difference in the aims stated in Paris and the commitments voluntarily subscribed to by governments. Thus, no market rules for carbon[3] after 2020 have been established and discussed. The risk of the current situation involves an increase of temperature by more than 3°C. The idea that environmental protection can slow down growth, penalize employment, and impoverish people has become commonplace. This would be true if, in addition to investment in renewable energy, electric cars, and sustainable technology, there were no investments to support those who were adversely affected by reducing fossil fuels.

Presented in Geneva in 2019, the Special Report on Climate Change and Land of the Intergovernmental Panel on Climate Change stresses that more or less a quarter of greenhouse gas derives from bad soil use. Thus, we must reduce deforestation, increase afforestation/reforestation, practice more sustainable agriculture, and consume less land because field irrigation corresponds to 70% of the human use of freshwater. So, too, we must adopt a balanced diet, featuring plant-based food, such as whole grains, legumes, fruits, and vegetables, the growing of which results in fewer carbon dioxide emissions and consume little red meat, which produces greenhouse gas from animal excrement in massive breeding farms.[4] The report calculates that 25–30% of food is lost or wasted: from 2010 to 2016, this contributed to 8–10% of the total amount of worldwide greenhouse gas emissions.

At the 2019 UN Climate Change Conference in Madrid, about 200 countries jointly decided how to improve strategies to combat global warming that were adopted before the Kyoto Protocol and the Paris Agreement that was to start in 2020. The main measures for reaching the goal of zero emissions by 2050 were:

- Renouncing fossil fuels and substituting them with renewable sources, such as wind and solar power
- Deciding the amount of funds for developing countries, more affected by global warming than other countries
- Revising transportation plans at every level through a plan of decarbonization and the development of electric vehicles
- Improving the efficiency of the energy distribution through so-called smart grids (digital network intelligence).

Unfortunately, no agreement was reached on the practical measures that must be adopted to reach the goal. This demonstrates how these significant issues are underrated.

COP26 in Glasgow in 2021 has produced tentative results. While the US and Europe reconfirmed the 2050 target date for achieving carbon neutrality, Russia and China announced a zero emissions target for 2060 and India for 2070. 105 countries have committed to reducing global emissions of methane, a greenhouse gas responsible for a quarter of global warming since pre-industrial times, by at least 30% by 2030. Several countries have pledged to stop financing fossil fuels abroad. States most vulnerable to climate change highlighted that rich countries' emissions are historically much higher and called for the adoption of an "Emergency Climate Pact," calling for a sharp increase in funding to support the economies of developing countries. Finally, an agreement was reached to commit to halting deforestation by 2030. In the final declaration, the objectives of the Paris agreement were reaffirmed, i.e. to continue efforts to limit the increase in the earth's temperature to 1.5°C. But according to the experts, these are only good intentions without any rigorous commitments. While everyone agreed on the text, India and China got the term "phase-out" replaced by "phase-down" of fossil fuels.

We continue to witness the emergence of diseases that, like anxious travelers, migrate from the original tropical areas, that is, from distant and poor countries, in which they are endemic, to new areas in which they adapt. Today, it is not necessary to go to Africa to contract malaria or, less dramatically, to swim in the Atlantic or Indian Ocean and to encounter colorful fish swimming with gray sea bass, which are disoriented, more or less like humankind, following an alien invasion (Preta, 2019b).

We humans are more or less 7 billion (we were 1 billion and 600,000 in 1900) in number, and it is a plausible estimate that we will reach 9 billion by the middle of this century. There are too many people in the world. Thus, the increasing population growth, in spite of the difference in number from country to country, puts natural resources at risk of excessive exploitation.

In spite of the significant progress in the past 15 years, few people can access clean water. In 2015, 3 people out of 10 (2 billion and 1 million) did not have access to drinking water and 6 out of 10 (4.5 billion) did not have toilets.[5] In 2020, Pope Francis stressed that no one is saved alone and condemned the radical individualism and the globalization of indifference.

Environmental pollution kills more or less six million people every year. Nine million people prematurely died because of contaminated water and air pollution in 2015, according to a paper published in the journal *The Lancet* (Landrigan et al., 2017). Exposure to contaminated air, water, and soil kills more people than obesity, alcoholism, malnutrition, and traffic accidents. Children are more at risk than adults: brief exposure to chemical substances in utero and early childhood causes chronic conditions, disabilities, and death.

A child died every four seconds because of poor environmental conditions, according to the Global Environment Outlook, according to a report written by 250 scientists from 70 countries and presented at the UN Environmental Assembly in 2019. Today, people are 60% more likely to leave their country because it is subjected to progressive desertification provoked by extreme meteorological events than they were 40 years ago. There are about 25.3 million so-called environmental immigrants, according to the International Organization for Migration. They will outnumber 143 million in 2050, according to one estimate. The number of climate refugees – those who must emigrate because of the rise in the sea level caused by melting glaciers and an increase in water temperature, all factors eroding entire coasts – is triple the number of war refugees. Their numbers continuously increase. Environmental factors accounted for 9% of migrations of the past decade. This is because the very survival of indigenous people directly depends on a balanced ecosystem. People who escape environmental disasters are forced to live in hiding and poverty: they are often perceived as the universal enemy, the Freudian hostile, whose only fault is his mere presence, which threatens Western well-being.

Access to safe drinking water and sanitation was recognized as a human right in 2010,[6] but it is not a reality for all. Many world movements to recognize this as a fundamental human right are on the rise, in opposition to the global grabbing[7] of precious resources. Contaminated water endangers some communities, making people less resistant to viruses and bacteria. The consequences include death, male and female infertility, and neurocerebral developmental damage to children.

Various disciplines, among them sociology, anthropology, political philosophy, philosophy of science, psychology, architecture, city planning, climatology, and environmental science, support the validity of ecological themes. More specifically, these disciplines support the need to sustain the right to climate balance, the conservation of the planet's resources, the value of biodiversity,[8] the use of alternative energy, such as wind and solar power, and the fight against food waste[9] and planned obsolescence.[10] This would necessitate reusing, repurposing, recycling, and ending the environmental degradation of our soil, coastlines, oceans, and seas. Otherwise, garbage-laden barges will continue to move across our oceans and seas, plastic bags will continue to suffocate dolphins and birds, masses of microplastics[11] will continue to degrade the health of the water,[12] already damaged by acidification and trawling.

We must oppose the deterioration of nature and biodiversity, on land and in water, for example, the indiscriminate deforestation, the rising sea levels damaging coasts, the progressive destruction of barrier reefs, the rapid reduction and extinction of a multitude of animal and plant species that maintain the biosphere's equilibrium.

So, too, we must stop the endless extraction[13] and excessive use of fossil fuel and, its consequence, the increase in greenhouse gases emissions, in particular, CO_2,[14] lest we continue creating environmental disasters, such as floods and making heat waves hotter and cold fronts colder.

It is crucial to recognize these issues, from the widespread dryness of the soil, which can mean possible conflicts between farmers and breeders for more fertile land and the consequent decrease in food production to the abuse of pesticides and illegal growth stimulators for plants. The latter contaminates our food but gives it an aesthetically pleasing look, leading us to confuse the "good" with the "beautiful," the pleasure of the body with that of the eyes.[15] Further, they kill bees and other helpful pollinators.

Climate change, especially extreme cases such as glaciations and deglaciations, has always existed in the history of Earth. However, such change has never occurred as rapidly as it is today. In *Ice: Tales from a Disappearing Continent* (Ghiaccio. Viaggio nel continente che scompare) (2019), the glaciologist Marco Tedesco, one of the leading figures on climate change, and the journalist Alberto Flores D'Arcais describe how Greenland, the land of ice, is threatened by the rising sea level, the crazy march of polar bears toward the hinterland in search of food, and the easy navigation of some routes, such as the Northwest Passage, which were once considered impossible to traverse.

Ron Giblett (2019) is right to consider as "psychogeopathologies" or "environmental psychopathologies" environmental ills, such as water scarcity, air pollution, and uncontrolled urbanization. The responsible thing to do is to find a new equilibrium for redefining the unlimited development of the 20th and 21st centuries,[16] to avoid the butterfly effect, that is, a moving of molecules produced by the flapping of a butterfly's wings that can trigger a chain of other moving molecules that ultimately lead to a far-off hurricane. The butterfly effect metaphor perfectly describes how, in a complex system, such as our environment, minimal variations can produce enormous consequences.

Notes

1 In an 1896 article, the Swedish chemist Svante Arrhenius (1859–1927) calculates that the double increase of CO_2 in the atmosphere would lead to a rise of 5–6°C. Perhaps naively, Arrhenius argues that industrial fossil fuel consumption would benefit agriculture, thanks to the Greenhouse effect, and Stockholm's temperature would drop. However, he also calculates that this would take millennia: he could not predict the enormous increase in fossil fuel use in the 20th century. Freud was extremely attentive, curious about the popularization of science, and he had in his London library the German edition (1908) of the book by Svante Arrhenius, Nobel Prize winner for chemistry in 1906, on global warming (Trosman and Simmons, 1973). That said, Leonardo da Vinci foresaw the problem of global warming half a millennium ago in his Codex Arundel. He described an arid Earth, dried out by the sun to the point where living beings and nature are extinguished. Named after its first recognized owner, Henry Howard XXIII, Earl of Arundel, it is a collection of 283 drawings and writings dated between 1478 and 1518. It is preserved at the British Library in London.

2 In 2021, under the Biden administration, the United States rejoined the Paris Agreement.

3 This is *International Emissions Trading*. The states that adhered to the Kyoto Protocol agreed to respect the aims of limitation/reduction of greenhouse gas emissions. These aims are measured in "assigned amount units." The emissions trading permits parties to save their units (that is, choose to not use some of their assigned emissions) and sell them to parties that exceed theirs.

4 Jonathan Safran Foer (2009, 2019) considers the topic of our diet and so of the strong reduction of consumption of animal products for countering greenhouse gas emissions. In his 2019 book, he argues that, on the one hand, changing our diet per se cannot save the planet but, on the other, we cannot save the planet without changing our diet.

5 This data is from the World Water Development Report entitled *"Leaving No One Behind,"* published on World Water Day, March 22, 2019.

6 In 2010, at the suggestion of some Latin American countries, the United Nations General Assembly, and subsequently the Human Rights Council approved two important resolutions sanctioning the right to water and sanitation as a universal, human, autonomous, and specific right: an essential human right toward the quality of life and the exercise of all human rights.

7 This refers to the phenomenon of international conglomerates acquiring water sources.

8 By encouraging farmers to produce more at a lower price instead of improving the quality of food, industrial agriculture is responsible for the loss of global biodiversity. We must move to a diversified and sustainable agro-ecological system. From the mid-1900s onward, agrochemical and agricultural biotechnology corporations have been developing and patenting genetically modified seeds. These corporate giants, which often also produce pesticides and herbicides, create a destructive imbalance in agricultural systems and force farmers to buy their supplies in a dependency cycle: entire supply chains become fragile by abandoning native crops. The European Parliament spoke out against such patents in September 2019. It proposed a motion that stressed that because plant and animal varieties are biological processes, their products cannot be patented.

9 A 2006 French law permits supermarkets with an area of over 400 square meters to sign an agreement with charities to which to donate unsold products, obtaining tax incentives in exchange. In 2019, this obligation was extended to restaurants, public and private canteens, and small food stores. This law and its

extension attempt to solve the problem of food waste, which occurs in private homes and represents 40% of total waste.

10 Another French law will oblige commercial activities to donate all unsold products to charity by 2023. Repair services are favored, especially those for household appliances. Businesses will have to put label on goods with their expected life span. This is to enter into force in all European Union countries in 2021 and oblige industry to make available spare parts for at least seven years after a product is sold.

11 Microplastics are very small parts of plastics, whose size varies between 330 µm and 5 mm, coming from the degradation of larger plastic objects in the sea due to wind, wave motion, or ultraviolet light. Plastic filaments can be difficult to distinguish from plankton and therefore are ingested by sea organisms, fishes, and mollusks. Thus, they can represent a risk for the consumption of fish products. Furthermore, microplastics can provide support for the proliferation of colonies of pathogenic microbes (Greenpeace, 2016).

12 The Pacific Trash Vortex or Great Pacific Garbage Patch, a floating collection of marine debris, is estimated to be up to twice the size of Texas (Moore and Phillips, 2011). Another comparable mass of floating debris is the North Atlantic Garbage Patch. Van Aken (2020) points out that this patch is a sort of isle that appears as something both familiar (our plastic is so typical of our world and constitutes our modernity) and "uncanny," that is, frightening and shapeless. It is something both solid and fluid, both enormous and dusty. It can recombine itself through sea mixing and becomes a new polymorphic, elusive, and socially unthinkable reality. This plastic isle is a paradigm of what is unthinkable in terms of the nature–culture dichotomy and thus of the way through which we give an order to the world. For this reason, it is an absolute and menacing impurity: it is both familiar and stranger, phantasmatic and uncanny.

13 Fracking or hydraulic fracturing is a process of extracting oil and natural gas from shale rocks. This is obtained through injecting a toxic mixture of water, sand, and chemicals at very high pressure into the subsoil. It causes the emergence of oil and natural gases on the surface. Fracking is much more expensive than traditional drilling and has the following environmental consequences:

  1 Consumption of the water brought in the exploration sites.
  2 Risk of contaminating aquifers around the extraction areas with toxic substances, as only 80% of the injected liquid returns to the surface as reflux water, while the rest remains underground.
  3 Triggering minor earth tremors.

Many European countries, including Italy, do not permit fracking and wait to better understand its environmental consequences.

14 Airplanes are particularly polluting as they produce CO_2 faster than other sources of greenhouse gas. Air travel is a blind spot among environmental issues. For example, in France, only 15 National Assembly deputies proposed to abolish short-haul domestic flights. Teen environmental activist Greta Thunberg (2020) argues that an economy class passenger making the roundtrip from Stockholm to Tokyo produces 5.14 tons of CO_2. According to the World Bank, the average emissions of one inhabitant of India is 1.7 tons per year. In Bangladesh, it is 0.5 tons. Unfortunately, today we have neither engines nor alternative kinds of fuels. Nonetheless, an experiment of electric engines has been scheduled for the next ten years, as well as an experiment of light crafts flying without fuel.

15 Here the prototype is the poisoned apple that the wicked stepmother gives Snow White in the Brothers Grimm tale and Walt Disney's perfect visual representation (*Snow White and the Seven Dwarfs*, 1937). The poisoned apple's illusory and

seductive aspect masks its negative essence and the risks related to its symbolic value. Europe discards an estimated 3.7–51.5 million tons of fruit and vegetables each year, deeming it unsuitable for consumption because it does not meet the aesthetic and commercial standards of European norms, according to research by Porter et al. (2018). Growing the discarded food generates an annual mean of 22 million tons of CO_2.

16 Paul Virilio (in Binswanger, 2005) argues that we cannot clearly distinguish between natural and industrial or technological disasters. He posits that from the 20th century on, we have been in the era of the "integral accident," in which a single disaster or accident can potentially affect the entire world.

Chapter 2

Human beings and the environment[1]

In his novel *Qualcosa, Là Fuori* (Something Outside) (2016), Bruno Arpaia describes the feeling of surprise we felt upon first confronting the issue of environmental crime. This dangerous emergency is provoked by unexpected changes whose responsibility is difficult to recognize because its deleterious effects are often involuntary consequences of human activities, anthropocentrism, and, sometimes even, our good intentions.

Surprise ought not to be the reaction given the scientific information that is available to us today[2] and the clear and exhaustive assessment of this global predicament should have made us quite aware of the effects of Anthropocene.[3]

Ecological ethics posits that there are good reasons to be alarmed. We cannot be ingenuously optimistic or irresponsibly indifferent toward the limitations of Earth's natural resources, though we too often consider them unlimited.

In his pamphlet *Il Grido* (The Shout) (2018), Antonio Moresco presents a sort of night of humankind to denounce our having chosen a mass suicide of sorts, an extinction, toward which we appear indifferent and which we repress at the political, economic, social, cultural, and individual levels. Moresco appeals to us to use our capacity to invent, quoting Albert Einstein's famous sentence, according to which *"we cannot solve our problems with the same thinking we used when we created them."*[4]

As an alternative to anthropocentrism, we should consider all plants as being similar to a nation possessing a constitution[5] based on general principles that rule the community of living beings and coexist with all species, not only humans. Thanks to photosynthesis, plants produce all the free oxygen in our planet and all the chemical energy consumed by other living beings. We exist, thanks to plants, and we can continue to exist only with them (Mancuso, 2019).

Following *Walden; or, Life in the Woods* (1854) by Henry David Thoreau, perhaps the first ecological novel, in *The Overstory* (2018), Richard Powers describes a natural world that seems frail but that is actually strong and longstanding. He highlights how plants and forests are important for the

DOI: 10.4324/9781003220077-3

equilibrium of the planet and how human beings are so narcissistically self-centered that they do not give them and their gifts much importance. It is as if human beings consider themselves superior to other forms of life and value only what resembles them. Powers argues that the main problem with people is that life seems to run alongside them. There is the soil and the cycle of water. Ingredients are traded. Weather happens and the atmosphere exists. Nature feeds, cures, and shelters many more types of creatures than people know how to count.

Bruno Latour (2015) is against the repression of the interdependencies and focuses on the concept of "habitable planet," according to which every living organism creates the life conditions for others. In Gaia, there is nothing intentional, harmonious, or providential: there is only a useful interaction among the life conditions of the various organisms populating it.

Recent studies have shown that the genes do not move only in a vertical direction, that is, from one generation to the next one, but also in a lateral direction. This means that they can go beyond the boundaries of a specific species and pass from a realm to another. These studies try to clarify the phylogenetic relationships among all beings living on Earth and put some disturbing questions on the concepts of species and individual (Quammen, 2018).

Manuela Monti and Carlo Alberto Redi (2019) invented the term "co-individual" to indicate that the biological individual is a heterogeneous set of organisms, a symbiosis of forms in constant metamorphosis and relationship with their environment.

With great intellectual honesty, Freud stresses his difficulty in maintaining an objective perspective on events strongly involving him during the First World War. This is how he opens the essay *Thoughts for the Time on War and Death* (1915, p. 275):

> In the confusion of wartime in which we are caught up, relying as we must on one-sided information, standing too close to the great changes that have already taken place or are beginning to, and without a glimmering of the future that is being shaped, we ourselves are at a loss as to the significance of the impressions which press in upon us and as to the value of the judgments which we form. We cannot but feel that no event has ever destroyed so much that is precious in the common possessions of humanity, confused so many of the clearest intelligences, or so thoroughly debased what is highest. Science herself has lost her passionless impartiality; her deeply embittered servants seek for weapons from her with which to contribute towards the struggle with the enemy. Anthropologists feel driven to declare him inferior and degenerate, psychiatrists issue a diagnosis of his disease of mind or spirit. Probably, however, our sense of these immediate evils is disproportionately strong, and we are not entitled to compare them with the evils of other times which we have not experienced.

With the same intellectual honesty as Freud, today we can claim to know enough about the negative consequences of the present model of development and the outcomes of environmental negligence. We are induced to not recognize our dependence on the biosphere, but we have many valid ways of knowing and assessing our emotional ambiguities.

According to Michel Foucault (1984), going back at least to the time of Ancient Greece, we have had a constant and detailed focus on the problem and the differential valorization of environment in relationship to the body. Environmental elements are perceived as bearing positive or negative effects on health. We postulate that so complex a web of interferences between us and our surroundings make it possible that a simple juncture, a certain situation, or a minimal change in the order of things can provoke morbid states in the body.

For some time now, the World Health Organization has been reporting the clear connection between the emergence of a grave pandemic such as the COVID-19 outbreak in 2020 and the relationship between environment and health in general and, more specifically, the global system of food production, urbanization, factory farming, deforestation, destruction of habitats – all things that force animals, in particular wild ones, to adapt to new conditions and thus become more prone to spreading pathogens. Similar considerations are found in David Quammen's *Spillover* (2012). This book about the evolution of pandemics, describes, in addition to the factors mentioned above, how travel in areas previously inaccessible to humans provoked the transmission of certain zoonotic infections. The term "spillover" refers to when a virus is transmitted from its non-human host (an animal) to the first human host who then travels around the world and infects other people, going from zoonosis to pandemic.

The measures that the Chinese government adopted to prevent the spread of COVID-19 lessened carbon consumption. That, along with a significant drop in air transportation, reduced CO_2 emissions. The same happened in countries that saw a drastic reduction in industrial production and vehicle and air traffic. Although registered in a crisis, this demonstrates that large-scale action against CO_2 emissions can be very effective. Thus, in a certain sense, the COVID-19 pandemic can be considered as a test on our realistic capacity to counter the climate crisis. A few months, which is less than a moment in cosmic terms, are sufficient for the ecosystem to begin to recover from the damage that human beings have been inflicting upon it. The waters of our rivers and seas have become more transparent; the sky has slowly lost its gray color that we are used to and turned blue; some animals that we would have never imagined seeing in our cities have been wandering on the streets empty of cars. It is important to give value to these environmental results and to create ecological transition at every level. Biodiversity must be protected and renewable energies must be promoted instead of fossil fuels. This will lead to mechanisms of production that are less polluting and harmful than those used in the past.

Amitav Ghosh (2016) defines our era as that of the great derangement. There has never been an era in which the forces of weather and geology either exerted so strong an influence over our lives or pressed themselves on us so directly and relentlessly.

I believe it is crucial and urgent for the various cultural and scientific fields to find a way toward dialogue, sometimes polemically, if we are to avoid each field limiting itself in self-referential and obtuse specialism.

Also those scientific disciplines that should shed some light on social events are characterized by narcissistic individualism and fragmentation. This is similar to what Ferenczi called "confusion of tongues" (Mappa, 2020).

Further, strongly defending the urgency to find environmental balance does not mean accepting something akin to the anti-universalistic utopia of the degrowth proposed by Serge Latouche (2007), whose germs can be found in utopian socialists[6] of the early 20th century such as Henri de Saint-Simon, William Morris, Charles Fourier, and Robert Owen. A common thread for these thinkers is a nostalgic and utopian return to rural and artisan simplicity. What I propose in this book does not support this utopian perspective: rather, I aim to preserve the common good and give value to beauty in all its forms by constructing defined ecological change. In this sense, innovation can be a tool for responsible action, a tool that values the integrity of ecosystems without altering their delicate balance.

For Luciano Floridi (2020), a human ethical project consisting of green environmentalism and blue digital policies is necessary. This project must support a politics of experience and not of consumption and waste, that is, based on the qualities of the relationships and processes and not on material things and their possession.

In the words of Freud (1930, p. 82), *"Beauty has no obvious use; nor is there any clear cultural necessity for it. Yet civilization could not do without it."*

Beyond beauty, we must value psychophysical well-being and the future of our children and grandchildren. This is only possible by avoiding those denials, those psychic fossilizations, which are widely present in us and transmitted to the next generation. We cannot reproduce our planet.[7] The damages we have wrought are sort of bankrupting our descendants. Generational transmission implies an identification process that summarizes a history that, for the most part, does not belong to future generations. When we underestimate the contract that links everyone to the whole and vice versa – us to Earth and Earth to us – we necessarily transmit symptoms, defense mechanisms, organization in object relations, the signifiers, all the elements in which the forms and processes of the psychic reality of a single subject articulated with the forms and processes that constitute intersubjective relationships, and, more in general, our relationship with our environment (Kaës, 1993).

The word "ecology" originally defined the branch of biology dealing with the relationships between living organisms and the environment. Later, it applied to activities affecting the environment in terms of sustainability and, subsequently, to environmental damage.

Ecology must not only deal with the defense of animals or the effects of global warming but must also offer a general framework for countering problems, such as land degradation, caused by some kinds of cultivation or factory farming. This would create a better future for the individual, society, and humankind (Morin, 2016).

Masud Khan (1983) starts from the Oxford English Dictionary definition of the noun "fallow: *"ground that is well-ploughed and harrowed but left uncropped for a whole year or more."* He uses the evocative image of fallow fields that farmers leave to rest and to remain fruitful. In the analytic relationship, the metaphor of lying fallow indicates a transitional state of experience, a mode of being alert but quiet, as well as receptive with regard to consciousness. Lying fallow is proof that a person can be alone without any purpose.

The human being needs the Earth and the Earth needs the human being; therefore, it is essential to be open to exchanges with other elements of cultural and biological ecosystems.

In his *Prolegomena to a Third Surrealist Manifesto or Not* (1942), André Breton writes that the human being is not the center or the focal point of the Universe. We can go so far as to believe that there exists beyond human beings, on the animal scale, beings whose behavior is as strange to them as theirs may be to the mayfly or the whale.

It is a cultural resource to be open to the analysis of relationships to those subjects that are interdependent, that is, that mix from which every culture has originated different creative forms. If we take a general look at the network of nature and culture that allows us to inhabit our cities, relate to things, illuminate, drink, love a certain place, all of a sudden, our interdependence emerges, and, at the same time, we are able to connect with the environments of our life and give them new meanings and practices (Van Aken, 2020).

Pope Francis (2015) contextualizes respect for the environment in ethical and aesthetical terms. He underscores the preeminence of mankind's right to beauty, so distant from the ideological and aesthetic pauperism found in some of the literature of the Catholic Church.

Repairing cities

Pope Francis (2015) criticizes unlimited growth, noting that many cities have grown in a disproportionate and unhealthy manner not only due to air pollution but also because of inadequate transportation and visual and noise pollution. Congestion and lack of green space befall not just old cities but new ones, too. For Pope Francis, people cannot live surrounded by asphalt, glass, and metal, with no contact with nature.

Ronald Laing (1969) argues that our surrounding environment can offer many positives or severely reduce them – and this is the main meaning humans give to architecture. The splendor of Athens, as Pericles viewed it, and the horror of so many modern megalopolises is that the former widened human awareness, whereas the latter dimmed it.

Cities do not grow according to quasi-natural rules. Cities are not only physical realities organized according to social and economic factors: they possess a psychological and anthropological dimension; they are the result of a mix of the conscious and unconscious; they share much with dreams. To render our cities expressions of selves, the participation and expectations of the entire community are essential. It is nothing short of a tragedy that our governments have forgotten this (Rykwert, 1963, 2000).

When we travel through a city or we stroll through our neighborhood, every glance at a compelling object can produce a moment of reverie. This is because cities are unconscious processes. From aesthetics to local interests to economics, a multitude of functions influence and contrast one another. In this sense, cities mirror the apparent chaos of our unconscious mind, they resemble an ordinary person with his biological, sexual, historical, spiritual, professional, familial, and economic interests. All these aspects are bonded in a moving form that gives rise to a certain perspective (Bollas, 2000).

Maurizio Corrado (2012) brings a unique perspective to the discussion that architecture must be at the service of green space and not the other way around. Here, green space is considered basic or fundamental, not optional or redundant. Corrado does not advocate the mere construction of new gardens, rather something radical: a city that includes a forest. This forest is not a dangerous place, a threat to the city's security. This forest provides something elementally important to the city – a clearing, a vast meadow surrounded by trees, an urban prairie teeming with herbs and flowers. This carries more than an aesthetic value: eliminating the border between natural areas and buildings improves the quality of the air and the ability of the soil to absorb water.

In a recent interview (Gallione, 2019), Stefano Boeri presents *A Green River*,[8] a reforestation project that would create 35 kilometers of green areas and 1.5 million square meters of new parks in Milan by redeveloping defunct railway stations, railway tracks, parking lots, and school courtyards. This would be the engine for the city's future urban and environmental development. Trees, urban forests, roofs, green building facades, and the integration of vegetation in architecture in cities such as Milan would connect to the Apennine Mountains and the Alps, creating a great green unified infrastructure connecting the Italian Peninsula.

The behavior of the cities is not so different from that of living beings. Thus, it is mandatory to appeal more to plants than to animals when we talk about cities. In fact, like plants, cities do not move but rather grow up. Plants are not greedy for resources as animals because they are energetically autonomous. In this sense, we must consider plants to imagine new solutions for an ecological and energetically sustainable growth of cities (Mancuso, 2020).

In recent years, we have seen a tendency to promote sustainable architecture, planned according to the global well-being of inhabitants and the environment surrounding them. This can be done also by applying bioclimatic principles to passive architecture, utilizing local renewable sources. Buildings and architecture can greatly reduce energy consumption.

For Michelangelo Russo (2016), contemporary architecture adheres to an eco-systematic idea, with new and clear relationships between the city, environment, and landscape, in various contexts. It involves various innovative forms of action (through ideas such as recycling) and social and interactive practices (cooperation, co-habitation, co-working, and new ways supporting cultural and ethnic pluralism).

This is a dynamic movement at the physical, emotional, and social levels that values the relationship between the human mind and habitation. It aims to build its unitarity by harmonizing two vital functions: the defense of our intimacy and our need to stay in touch with others and our surrounding environment.

The continuous repairing and active maintenance of cities is nothing short of absolutely necessary (Sennett, 2018).

Renzo Piano proposes building new structures over what is already built. He calls this "mending of urban suburbs," so as to avoid transforming urban areas into a great no man's land (Merlo, 2018).

The term "mending" involves loving interventions that improve the suburbs, which he calls "border areas," which invoke imagination and desire. That is where we find those lives at the border of life that, for this reason, represent life more than life itself does. The suburbs are the cities we will build and bequeath, which tell something about us.

In *Site Planning* (1962), Kevin Lynch and Gary Hack outline how to recover soil and how to re-use abandoned areas such as railway stations, pasture, and floodplains. About three decades later, Kevin Lynch (1990) stresses the importance of wild urban areas and abandoned places in which children can discover adventure and freedom.

Vito Cappiello (2017) invites landscape architects to go beyond the idea of embellishment that is common in planning landscape so as to explore the transformation of the so-called "black holes" of the contemporary city. We must change our perspective about such abandoned, rejected places if we are to cease wasting our landscapes' resources (energy, material, aesthetics, etc.).

Duccio Demetrio (2005) asks us to pay attention to falsifications and proposes authentic city planning instead of urban pseudo-reparative embellishments, such as better pedestrian areas, which cannot ameliorate the livability of urban areas.

These urban areas are at the center of Patrick Ravignant's novel *The Cities of the Bald* (1960), which describes the conformism of "cities of the bald," so defined because they are made of reinforced concrete and bitumen and because their few green areas try to hide their desolation as does an ugly wig on a bald head. City planning proposals that appear to promote ecology but that are actually insufficient, hasty, and foster degradation are not unusual.[9] They are false and artificial; they do not consider the general planning of the city, and they avoid going to the core of problems, which persist and increase.

Demetrio's warning also applies to all those propagandistic operations that promote pseudo-repair, that instead of concretely reducing environmental damage, actually hide it with cosmetics or even cause new damage.

Thinking about future generations

According to the Talmud (Taanit 23a), Honi HaMe'agel, the legendary circle drawer, was walking in the street when he saw a man planting a carob tree. Honi asked him, "How long does it take for the carob to bear fruit?" The man answered, "More or less 70 years." Honi further asked him, "Are you sure that you will live another 70 years?" The man answered, "I found already grown carob trees in the world. My forefathers planted them for me. Thus, I, too, plant these for my children."

Karl Marx (1867) exhorts treating soil as perpetual property of the collectivity. This is an unalienable right of future generations. Marx grasps the essence of the contemporary idea of sustainable development, whose most famous definition is found in the conclusion of the Brundtland Report (*Our Common Future*)[10]: "*Sustainable development is development that meets the needs of the present without compromising the ability of future generations to meet their own needs.*"

Similarly, Hans Jonas (1979) argues that, according to the principle of responsibility, we must have a meaningful perspective that goes beyond our single lives. Our successors have the right to expect a world in at least not a condition worse than in which we found it. His ecological imperative is for us to act so that the consequences of our actions allow for genuine human life.

Gunther Anders (1980) warns us about the fact that a sort of uncontrolled technology can prevail over our power of doing, predicting, and assessing the consequences.

So, too, Gustavo Zagrebelsky (2017) opposes intergenerational prevarications: he posits that we have the duty to moderately use resources and the obligation to respect the rights of future generations, because the choices of parents inevitably influence the lives of their children. Future generations have no obligation toward the previous ones, but previous ones have duties toward the future ones. In this sense, if we speak of the right to life of the conceived person, we mean the duties of the pregnant woman. The responsibility toward those who will come after us cannot be separated from the way we live our lives. If we rape nature and make Earth unbearable and infertile, we destroy living beings, we reduce humankind to a passive, ignorant, manipulated, and manipulable mass, and we hurt ourselves. Present and future are inexorably connected. The main task of living beings is to preserve the conditions for biological life and its freedom. This is for us and then for our children and also for the children of our children, without end.

A group of young people aged as young as nine years old filed a constitutional climate lawsuit against the U.S. government,[11] against the legal measures that destroy, endanger, and compromise the climate and the unalienable system that nature gave humankind. They claim that the U.S. government not only violated the rights of the young generation to life, freedom, and property but also failed in its duty to protect basic public resources.

The Trump Administration demanded the dismissal of the lawsuit, but the U.S. Supreme Court ruled unanimously in favor of the legitimacy of the young people's arguments.

Luc Magnenat (2019c) invites us to transmit, as *passeurs* (ferrymen who transport people and goods from one shore to the other), ecological ideals to future generations: there is a fundamental asymmetry between nature, which can exist without human beings, and human beings themselves who, if they continue to act in such a self-harming way, would impede future generations from benefiting from ecosystems that they benefited from yet also left them damaged.

These ideals are neither secondary aspects nor compensation to be paid to progress, but are fundamental features, integral and constitutive parts of progress itself. We must explore new forms of partnership with nature, no more possession and conquest: progress must be in terms of sustainability, not destruction.

Today more than ever, there cannot be social responsibility without environmental responsibility (Emery 2007).

To protect ecosystems and solve the dramatic consequences of environmental degradation, Pope Francis[12] (2015) advocates integral sustainable development and a cyclical model of production (regeneration, drastic reduction of waste and pollution, and reuse of materials). These actions must be linked to social justice to guarantee people's inclusion and participation and the present generation's right to a common destination of the soil's goods, but also the future generations', void of denial, indifference, resignation, or blind confidence in technical solutions. Nonetheless, he is optimistic of humankind's capacity to rebuild its common home.

The leaders of the October 2019 "Synod on the Amazon" asked the Catholic Church to release a formal document recognizing sins against the environment along with traditionally recognized sins.

The physicist Fritjof Capra (1982) opposes the Cartesian mechanistic conception of physics and proposes an organic, holistic, and ecological physics. He points out that, in modern physics, the idea of the universe as a machine has been challenged by the view of it as being indivisible and dynamic, in which its parts are interconnected and can be understood only as patterns of a cosmic process.

Capra and Mancuso (2019) consider the botany studies of Leonardo da Vinci, who promoted the idea of a living world that is interconnected and interdependent, an entrenched network of relationships and intimacies. They also consider Charles Darwin's observations in his work *On the Origin of the Species* (1859), which support the complexity of ecological links between living beings and warn that the consequences of intervention on these relationships[13] are unpredictable. Capra and Mancuso invite humankind to imitate plants' extraordinary capacity to create networks and cooperate. For example, trees are connected to and interact with nearby trees. In terms of resilience and innovative development, it follows that the idea of competition between individuals as the engine of progress should be substituted with that of cooperation and mutual support, typical of vegetation.

Powers (2018) considers these topics in narrative terms. He argues that something beautiful is occurring underground, something that we are becoming aware of now. Mats of mycorrhizal cabling connect trees in enormous and smart communities across hundreds of acres. All these trees take the form of vast networks of goods, services, and information. There are no single entities in a forest. Each cannot be separated from the others. The bird and the tree on which it sits on are connected. A third or more of the food a gigantic tree creates feeds many other organisms. Even different types of trees are in a partnership. If you cut down a birch, a nearby Douglas fir might suffer.

In *The Baron in the Trees* (1957), Calvino narrates the transgressive actions of Baron Cosimo Piovasco di Rondò. Cosimo, at the age of 12, after a quarrel with his father, decides to live out his life on trees, never to return to the ground. This novel can be seen as a castigation about our inability to value plants. Calvino describes the natural setting, the olive trees, the oaks, dense and thick, the pines giving way to chestnuts, the woods climbing up the mountain, trees as far as the eye can see. This is the universe in which Cosimo and his family live, hardly paying attention to it.

We call "common goods" the inorganic and organic elements of the biosphere without which humans would have no chance of survival: air, drinking water and sea water, fertile soil, food, flora, and fauna (Zagrebelsky, 2017).

Settis (2013), a staunch opponent of the devastation and destruction of the landscape, argues that "common good" means to develop a farsighted outlook, to invest in the future, to take care of the community of citizens, and to prioritize the young and their needs.

Thus, taking care of the common good demands that we strongly support the primary link between landscape and environment, avoid excessive and unruled exploitation of resources, recognize common needs between us and other species and forms of life such as animals, plants, minerals, with which we emphatically share Earth's resources. It means to refuse anthropocentric colonization and accept the irreducibility of the non-human to the human, of its autonomy.

In *Collapse* (2005), Jared Diamond accurately avoids any appeal to catastrophism and argues that ancient civilizations were able to reexamine the relationship with Earth as a system. They successfully faced environmental challenges and survived disasters. Contemporary civilization appears unable to do the same.

In *Steps to an Ecology of Mind* (1972), Gregory Bateson considers culture and progress in strongly ecological terms. In a study commissioned by the Hawaii Senate, he points out that three intertwined causes pose all present threats to the survival of mankind:

a   Technical progress, which cannot be avoided, but must be guided in the right direction;
b   Population growth, because the first condition for ecological stability is the balance between birth and mortality rates;
c   Errors in thoughts and attitudes in Western culture, such as our arrogance and hubris toward the natural environment.

Recognizing the inseparable link between us and the environment that provides us essentials, such as food, water, air, and energy, should compel us to improve global livability. Instead indifference, or, at worst, greed, and omnipotence continue to alter living conditions on Earth (Vassallo Torrigiani, 2014).

It is universally recognized that the environment is modified by the greenhouse effect and that this influences every aspect of our existence, from the reproductive success of the smallest plankton on the ocean surface to the survival of urban culture. One of the main features of entropy is its irreversibility, an increase of which translates into a decrease of available energy. This in turn creates pollution, a form of dissipation of energy accumulating in the environment and threatening the ecosystem and our health (Rifkin and Howard, 1980).

We must recognize that the culture of unlimited exploitation of natural resources, something that Freud himself considers, necessarily means a culture with mighty entropic growth (Emery, 2007). We are at a critical turning point in history: the old tools of civilization are both insufficient and unusable. Environmental entropy is so acute as to demand a new framework of energy resources that can create new technologies and new social, economic, and political institutions (Rifkin and Howard, 1980).

The crucial question at stake – a question that requires what psychoanalysis knows about collective and individual mental functioning – is why when mankind is well aware that its way of living endangers itself, yet seems wholly incapable of change. A person with this attitude would be considered crazy or suicidal (Magnenat, 2019a).[14]

A Danish proverb says that it is too late to learn to swim when the water is up to your lips.

Jean-Luc Nancy's answer (2014) is that we lost the capacity to learn from disasters and we are impotent when they repeatedly occur. Proof in this sense is what happened in Australia in 2019. In spite of a government-commissioned study predicting that global warming would soon cause devastating fires, rain, and drought, the anti-environment government and media spread many "fake news" stories assigning responsibility to pyromaniacs and environmentalist associations impeding firefighters from cutting down trees.

Diamond (2019) analyses momentous national crises to argue that, after a process of painful self-analysis and reflection about the future, individuals and groups can face present crises such as climate change. This should lead to a process of selective change because it is impossible to radically and entirely change past identity. Diamond proposes selectively assessing which parts of our individuality are working well and ought not to be modified and which parts require a change to discover new solutions in accordance with every person's capacities.

Jonathan Franzen (2019) assumes a radically pessimistic position: he argues that we can solve the dilemma between trying to avoid the inevitable climatic catastrophe and preparing to defend us against its negative effects by renouncing to invert the effects of global warming. We must focus on more easily achievable short-term goals through immediately feasible collective actions. These actions can allow us to have one less hurricane and a few more years of stability.

The only answer that can counter the impotence, inertia, and apathy that the present environmental disaster provokes in all of us, is to try to find and experiment with possible common remedies. This requires us to conceive humankind simultaneously as a collective and as single individuals.

Ferruta (2020) emphasizes the pleasure of personal responsibility and taking care of our conditions and of those who depend on us as an antidote against fear and indifference. The pleasure and capacity to emotionally experience trust in our caregivers allows us to discover unknown energies that can be used toward our good and the good of others.

In *Purgatorio* (XXII, 67–69), Dante Alighieri compares Virgil to an altruist who holds his lamp behind him and lights the way to make others wise, not himself.

We should do the same and shed light on those who walk behind us in the night. This holds the same for those who work not only for themselves but for those who follow as well, who help them learn and become experts.

Notes

1 All scientific data and estimates in this chapter are retrieved from https://www.un.org/en/sections/issues-depth/climate-change.

2 Science fiction often predicts ecological themes. For example, James G. Ballard foresees global warming in his novel *The Burning World*, published in 1964, at a time when these issues were not considered problematic. It is worth noting that Ballard's characters passively accept their precarious fate, spectators to the disaster, victims with no intention to act or ability to think.

3 The biologist Eugene F. Stoermer coined the term "Anthropocene" in the 1980s. The Nobel Prize Winner Paul Josef Crutzen reconsidered this term in 2000 to designate the present geological era in which the presence and activity of humans determines life conditions through global territorial, structural, and climatic modifications (Crutzen and Stoermer, 2000). The Anthropocene has yet to be recognized as a truly geological era distinct from the Holocene.

4 In *The New Quotable Einstein* (2005), editor Alice Calaprice indicates that this could be a paraphrase of Einstein's quote "A new type of thinking is essential if mankind is to survive and move toward higher level." That quote can be found in Michael Amrine's articles *"Atomic Education Urged by Einstein"* (The New York Times, May 25, 1946) and *"The Real Problem is in the Heart of Men"* (The New York Times Magazine, June 23, 1946).

5 In *Flower Power* (2020) Alessandra Viola proposes the First Universal Declaration of Plant Rights, similar to that of UNESCO's for animal rights. She argues that plants must be considered as living beings possessing dignity and autonomy, not as objects to preserve but legal entities.

6 Friedrich Engels (1880) defined utopian socialism in reductionistic terms when he compared it with scientific socialism.

7 The initiative Fridays for Future was organized by students and, until the COVID-19 pandemic, took place every Friday throughout the world. Spearheaded by Greta Thunberg, the first global strike for climate, Global Strike for Future, took place on March 15, 2019. Many environmental movements and scientists supported the strike and more than a million people demonstrated in 125 countries. The reasons for these protests are well documented in Thunberg's book *No One Is Too Small to Make a Difference* (2019).

8 Boeri's project seems to apply some rules of Judaism, which sets precise criteria for environmental protection (the "Migrash," a green belt around cities, the Sabbath giving land a rest, respect for fruit trees even during wartime).

9 Sandro Lagomarsini (2017) describes a misconception about trees planted in avenues: they are not "monuments in honor of nature;" trees that become part of a city must be controlled and maintained and, when necessary, cut down.

10 Retrieved from https://sustainabledevelopment.un.org/content/documents/5987our-common-future.pdf.

11 Details about this lawsuit can be found at https://www.ourchildrenstrust.org/juliana-v-us.

12 Pope Francis convened a special assembly of the Synod of the Bishops known as *Amazon: New Paths for the Church and for an Integral Ecology* in October 2019. Its focus was the Pan-Amazon Region, an area comprising nine South American countries and representing one of the planet's major biodiversity reserves (30–50% of the world's flora and fauna) and fresh water (circa 20% of non-frozen fresh water). Numerous large-scale economic interests threaten the richness of the Amazon, home to more than one-third of Earth's primary woods. There is rampant abuse by farmers cultivating soy and millet who burn the forest and by gold diggers and diamond hunters who contaminate rivers with mercury. The enormous growth of agriculture, extraction, and

deforestation damages not only the ecological richness of the region, but also its social and cultural reality. This demands that we resist the dominant culture of consumerism. The preparatory document from the synod specifies that there be a connection to other essential biomes: the Congo basin, the Mesoamerican biological corridor, the tropical forests of the Asian Pacific, the Guarani aquifer, among others. Leonardo Boff (2017) appeals to the figure of Chico Mendes, killed in 1988 as an archetype of the conservation of the Amazon forest and supporter of sustainability as a dynamic and self-regulating balance of Earth. Boff reconsiders his proposal to preserve forests by creating extractive reserves of natural products. By the way, these reserves seem to earn much more than deforestation. Deforestation of the Amazon increased by 88% from July 2018 to July 2019 under Brazilian President Jair Bolsonaro, according to the National Institute for Space Research, whereas 350 million trees were planted in Ethiopia by the Prime Minister and 2019 Nobel Peace Prize winner Abiy Ahmed.

13 In *The Descent of Man, and Selection in Relation to Sex* (1871), Charles Darwin stresses the importance of cooperation in the evolution of the species. He argues that societies that survive and develop are those whose members help each other. Animals that enjoy being together easily escape danger and have less of a chance of dying than those that are afraid of their peers and live alone.

14 In *The Art of Losing* (Zeniter, 2017) the main character's driver-guide in Algeria always keeps the car engine on, even when the car is stationary. Unconcerned about ecology, he says that in Algeria, gasoline costs nothing: it is the only luxury that Algerians can afford.

Chapter 3

Freud and the environment

Before defining his ideas about the controversial relationship between human beings and the environment in *Civilization and Its Discontents* (1930), Freud makes some extemporaneous notes about life in the city. He describes the city as full of conflicts, contradictions, and contrasts. Freud's considerations seem to parallel those of Georg Simmel in *The Metropolis and Mental Life* (1903), where he argues that, just as humans are not only defined by the boundaries of their body or of the space they occupy during an activity but also by the effects that they determine in time–space, so, too, a city can be defined by those effects that go beyond its immediacy.

Freud's early notes clearly anticipate his more articulated reflections about the discomfort of urban life and, more generally, of modern civilization and about the need to find a more harmonious contact with nature.

In his *The Life and Work of Sigmund Freud* (1953), Ernest Jones quotes Freud as saying regarding traveling in America: "America is a mistake; a gigantic mistake, it is true, but nonetheless a mistake" (p. 66). After visiting Coney Island, Freud calls it *"(…) a Prater seen through a magnifying glass (…),"* but when he sees Niagara Falls, he deems them *"(…) even grander and larger than he had expected"* (p. 4).

Clearly, during his visit to New York, Freud is not fascinated by the metropolis of "progress" and "freedom," by the city jungle, the city as spectacle (Ricci, 1995). Nonetheless, as an indication of the complexity of his opinions, Freud is fascinated, even a little intimidated, by the impetuosity of the falls, by the wildness of American nature, all things that will influence his future ideas about the relationship between human beings and nature.

In a postcard to his wife Martha from Genoa on September 13, 1905 (Tögel, 2002), Freud highlights the absence of green space in the city and draws some similarities with Viennese town planning: *"It is all made of stones, there are only streets like the Herrengasse and squares with buildings, then the harbor, some fortifications, the sea, the cemetery. Everything is extremely elegant, impressive, solid, almost defiant."*

DOI: 10.4324/9781003220077-4

Freud's opinions about Genoa and Vienna show an opposition without any apparent contradiction between his admiration for architectural beauty and elegance and his aversion for the lack of green space in cities (Schinaia, 2018).

The tendency toward the colossal but also the exuberance of wild nature in the United States, the lack of green space in architecturally elegant cities such as Vienna and Genoa, show Freud's great sensibility for urban planning, a sensibility not unidirectional, without prejudices. They partially anticipate the contents of *Civilization and Its Discontents.*

In various letters to his wife from various Alpine locations, Freud describes from a privileged perspective his relationship with a pure, idyllic, and authentically natural landscape. He does not cease to celebrate the beauty of the mountains of South Tyrol, Valtellina, and Engadina or to express his wonder for majestic landscapes and the emotions provoked by contemplating these immense panoramas.

In an August 13, 1898 letter to his wife (Tögel, 2002), Freud expresses his wonder for the incomparable glaciers, lakes, mountains, and sky during the journey from Pontresina to Maloja. In a September 14, 1900 letter to Wilhelm Fliess (Freud E. L., 1992) he describes the most beautiful coniferous forest and an unexpected solitude near Lavarone, an upland near Valsugana that can be reached through a walk on a mountain road of breathtaking beauty. Freud was so taken by the beauty of Lavarone that he would choose it for his holidays three times: in 1906, 1907, and 1923, staying for months in room 15 on the first floor of Hôtel du Lac.

Freud's typical day in Lavarone started with a three- or four-hour walk in the woods he described as splendid, in which he exercised the patience needed to observe and explore the events of nature. Freud wore the traditional Tyrolean costume: short pants with flashy suspenders and a green hat with a tuft of chamois beard, a walking stick with an iron tip and, in case of rain, a furry Alpine cape. In his explorations, he searched for mushrooms, blueberries, and strawberries, and he discovered and identified rare wildflowers.

In a 1913 photograph with his daughter Anna in South Tyrol, Freud seems to be relaxed as a holidaymaker. He appears very different from the romantic image we can find in Caspar David Friedrich's painting *Wanderer above the Sea of Fog* (1818). The wanderer of this painting is portrayed from behind, wearing a dark city overcoat. With wind-ruffled hair, he looks astonished and brooding as he watches the fascinating and sublime show of nature.

Another letter, addressed to his brother Alexander and dated September 17, 1909 (Tögel, 2002) on the letter head of the Grand Hotel Savoia informs us of Freud's stay in Rapallo. He describes a new way of relating to the environment. Freud was probably in Liguria to relax in a pleasant holiday, to swim in the sea, rather than to appreciate Genoa's Baroque palaces. Here are some passages that allow us to understand how Freud loved nature:

> (...) One just doesn't find time for anything; the heavenly sun and the divine sea – Apollo and Poseidon – are enemies of all mental activity. I realize that the only thing that has hitherto kept us going has been that remaining sense of obligation to identify – Baedeker in hand – new regions, museums, palaces, ruins; since this obligation does not exist here, I am simply drowning in a life of ease.
>
> Now for the sea. The beach is fine mud in which one can walk out for a quarter of an hour, head above water, and a little further on there are wonderful rocks (like those we saw in Capri) with pools in which one can sit, sloping carpets of rocks on which one rolls like a monster in one of Böcklin's pictures, completely alone and losing all account of time. Since I am all by myself I am not going in for serious fishing. But on the first day I managed to tickle an octopus, which refused to leave the water, then I got myself pricked by sea urchins, stung by jellyfish, tried in vain to detach some sea anemones and to catch some of those wily crabs whose legs here, too, are torn out by Italian urchins of the beach. The morning is taken up with bathing, which I find so much to my taste that next year I seriously making Viareggio (which I can't see this time) my sole aim. It is impossible to talk of the land unless one is a poet or quotes others. Everything grows here as in Sorrento except that there is a regular surfeit of palms, and one might well wonder about the merciful 'retribution'.
>
> (pp. 248–249)

In Rapallo, we are in Freud's garden, a place in which inactivity (otium) is a form of light intellectual activity, of cheerful and therefore effortless work, a game of fantastically playing with images and sensations (Ricci, 1995).

The holiday in the first years of the 20th century starts to become an integration and enrichment of the cultural Grand Tour, even among intellectuals who begin to conceive of nature without any idealization. Freud cannot be considered the new Goethe. He does not travel to the "land of lemons" and he does not feel any romantic *Sehnsucht* (grieving). Even if his heart points to the south, he does not seek a Mediterranean archetype contrasted and complementary to the Germanic one. Freud's interest in Southern Italy certainly comes from his desire to know and to learn, but it is also a middle-class need for holidays, an escape from urban stresses and the search for some relief from the nice summer resort (*Sommerfrische*) (Gnoli and Volpi, 2003).

In Freud, we have the city, culture, and the desire to know, as well as trekking in the mountains, bathing in the sea, and appreciating the beauty of the towns of the lakes of Garda, Como, and Maggiore, places far from Vienna where he finds temporary rest.

"Civilization and Its Discontents"

Civilization and Its Discontents (1930) is considered a starting point of many contemporary psychosocial analyses. Here, Freud argues that it is necessary to maintain individual limitations in the construction of civilization. Thus, he seems to put the basis of the ethics of collaboration and solidarity in which everyone must renounce something for the common good.

Freud writes (p. 95):

> The essence of it lies in the fact that the members of the community restrict themselves in their possibilities of satisfaction, whereas the individual knew no such restrictions.[1]

Further, he argues that (pp. 78 79) *"civilization (…) obtains mastery over the individual's dangerous desire for aggression by weakening and disarming it and by setting up an agency within him to watch over it, like a garrison in a conquered city."*

He adds (p. 146):

> The fateful question for the human species seems to me to be whether and to what extent their cultural development will succeed in mastering the disturbance of their communal life by the human instinct of aggression and self-destruction. (…) Men have gained control over the forces of nature to such an extent that with their help they would have no difficulty in exterminating one another to the last man. (…) And now it is to be expected that the other of the two 'Heavenly Powers,' eternal Eros, will make an effort to assert himself in the struggle with his equally immortal adversary.

Freud, similar to other thinkers such as Thomas Hobbes and Konrad Lorenz, considers man a fundamentally antisocial being who can be tamed only by the positive influence of society.

The renunciation of instinct is at the center of Freud's reflection on human relationships about the construction of modern civilization. However, he seemed not so strong in defining the relationship between man and the environment. Freud argued that man must protect himself from nature through technical mastery.

He wrote (p. 92):

> We recognize, then, that countries have attained a high level of civilization if we find that in them everything which can assist in the

exploitation of the earth by man and in his protection against the forces of nature – everything, in short, which is of use to him – is attended to and effectively carried out. In such countries rivers which threaten to flood the land are regulated in their flow, and their water is directed through canals to places where there is a shortage of it. The soil is carefully cultivated and planted with the vegetation which it is suited to support; and the mineral wealth below ground is assiduously brought to the surface and fashioned into the required implements and utensils.

For Freud, nature has a dominating strength, is wildly disorganized, and does not depend in any way on human will and intentions. For him, this is one of the main sources of human suffering, from which man, intimidated in their inevitable precariousness, will always have to protect themselves. There are some clear similarities with what Leopardi argued in his *Dialogue of Nature and an Icelander* (1824): a cruel and indifferent stepmother that can never be domesticated and friendly.

In *The Future of an Illusion* (1927a, p. 15) Freud pessimistically wrote:

> (…) She (the nature) destroys us coldly, cruelly, relentlessly, as it seems to us, and possibly through the very things that occasioned our satisfaction. It was precisely because of these dangers with which nature threatens us that we came together and created civilization (…). For the principal task of civilization, its actual raison d'être, is to defend us against nature.

Freud defined our relationship with nature as asymmetric and based on our attempts to maintain an illusory autonomy and control over chaos. In so doing he anticipated the tendency of Western civilization to consider the natural environment in conflictual and defensive way, that is, in terms of binary opposition. He referred to two paradigms, one regarding the dominions of man over nature and the other regarding the defense of man against a hostile nature. Both these paradigms are present throughout history and have strongly influenced the relationship between man and nature.

The defensive constructs of patriarchal civilization give to these infantile humane feelings of mastery that are only dangerous illusions of control (Dodds, 2011).

Freud continues (1927a, pp. 15–16):

> But no one is under the illusion that nature has already been vanquished; and few dare hope that she will ever be entirely subjected to man. There are the elements, which seem to mock at all human control: the earth, which quakes and is torn apart and buries all human life and its works; water, which deluges and drowns everything in a turmoil (…). With these forces nature rises up against us, majestic, cruel and inexorable;

she brings to our mind once more our weakness and helplessness, which
we thought to escape through the work of civilization.

Freudian anthropocentrism fits neatly into the Judeo-Christian tradition
and, specifically, the relationship between man and nature as it is transmitted from the Bible. In his commentaries of the Bible, Niccolò Scaffai
(2017) points out that in Genesis God gives man dominion over all things
and puts him at the center of a good and fruitful nature: (1:27) So God created humankind in his image, in the image of God He created them; male
and female He created them. (1:28) God blessed them and said to them, "Be
fruitful and multiply, and fill the earth and subdue it; and have dominion
over the fish of the sea and over the birds of the air and over every living
thing that moves upon the earth.") By giving a name to what he sees, Adam
had the privilege of ordering the nature that God created. Each living being,
with the exception of the tree of knowledge of good and evil, is determined
in its specificity and function by man and for man.

The banishment from the Garden of Eden radically reversed the natural environment, which turned from positive and advantageous to hostile
and impervious. Adam and Eve must now defend themselves from animals
and protect themselves from the cold. Scaffai stressed that what was offered
effortlessly must be obtained through work. After having lost original in-
nocence, man acquires a new skill: the ability to modify the environment
according to his needs through agriculture.[2]

The encyclical letter *Laudato Si'* (2015) proposes a less strong interpretation of the Bible: dominion over Earth (Genesis, 1:28) is an invitation
to cultivate and take care of the Garden of Eden (Genesis, 2:15). *"This
implies a relationship of mutual responsibility between human beings and
nature"* (p. 67).

Although I accept the specifications of the encyclical letter and the the-
ologian Enzo Bianchi's (2019) reference to those parts of the Bible inviting
the harmony between humankind and Earth, I agree with the Jungian analyst Mary-Jayne Rust (2008) that we must depart from both the interpretation of the myth of progress as Freud proposes and the interpretation
of the myth of the fall as the Bible proposes, that is, that nature banished
man for having eaten the fruit of the tree of knowledge. At this precise
moment in human history, we urgently need a myth that allows us to live
in harmony with nature and not against it, to live a life beneficial for all of
Earth's community.

In Freud's scientific-cultural proposal, humanity is depicted as a weak
and vulnerable child, defenseless against and frightened of a terrible, powerful, and uncontrollable Mother Nature, that Heraclitus conceived as that
immutable background that no God or man created. In these terms, civilization serves to defend us from its fury both in physical and psychological
terms.

It is worth noting that Freud's theorizing is not linear and sometimes appears contradictory. In fact, although in some parts he conceived man as an extension of God, in other parts, he wanted to mitigate human beings' need for absolute dominion over nature: *"(...) present-day man does not feel happy in his Godlike character"* (Freud, 1930, p. 92).

For example, Freud mitigates the apotheosis of technical development with the need to limit personal pleasure, as happened to prehistoric man when they renounced the childish desire to extinguish fire with urine:

> By damping down the fire of his own sexual excitation, he (the prehistoric man) had tamed the natural force of fire. This great cultural conquest was thus the reward for his renunciation of instinct.
>
> (Freud, 1930, p. 90)

Freud was fully aware that this was a conjecture and not a demonstrated historical fact. Nonetheless, he used such a conjecture to give imaginative strength to his thoughts. Further, he was able to relativize the glorification of technical development by alerting against its use for utilitarian aims (1930, pp. 92–94):

> (...) we welcome (...) as a sign of civilization as well if we see people directing their care too to what has no practical value whatever, to what is useless – if, for instance, the green spaces necessary in a town as playgrounds and as reservoirs of fresh air are also laid out with flower-beds, or if the windows of the houses are decorated with pots of flowers. (...) We require civilized man to reverence beauty[3] wherever he sees it in nature and to create it in the objects of his handiwork so far as he is able. (...) We expect besides to see the signs of cleanliness and order. (...) Dirtiness of any kind seems to us incompatible with civilization. (...) Beauty, cleanliness and order obviously occupy a special position among the requirements of civilization. (...) That civilization is not exclusively taken up with what is useful is already shown by the example of beauty, which we decline to omit from among the interests of civilization.

Freud's appreciation of beauty can be found also at the beginning of *On Transience* (1916b, pp. 305–306) when he lyrically describes a walk with a friend and a famous young poet

> (...) through a smiling countryside (...). As regards the beauty of Nature, each time it is destroyed by winter it comes again next year, so that in relation to the length of our lives it can in fact be regarded as eternal. (...) A flower that blossoms only for a single night does not seem to us on that account less lovely.[4]

Despite having written these notes in a historical and ecological context, which is radically different from the present one, Freud articulated a fundamental aspect of the experience related to the industrial changes of the 19th century and to their consequences and fears: the anticipatory mourning and the risk of the withdrawal of affection from those objects felt as damaged or damageable, that is, that mental condition that can find its expression in apathy. *On Transience* suggests that the environment and affectively invested objects can be experienced in a peculiar atmosphere of loss and fear of the end. The poet is only a passive witness of a possible future destruction and certainly experiences the mourning. But he does not work through the mourning: he uses a narcissistic defense to avoid the real and painful working through the mourning by anticipating it. In this sense, beauty is lost in advance. Freud does not accept this in any way and proposes to repair and recreate the internal and external world. He concluded his essay with these worlds (p. 307):

> When once the mourning is over, it will be found that our high opinion of the riches of civilization has lost nothing from our discovery of their fragility. We shall build up again all that war has destroyed, and perhaps on firmer ground and more lastingly than before.

Renee Lertzman (2013) argued that the position of the poet is the condition we know and classify as apathy or complacency. While it is impossible to know exactly what is going on in those who withdraw from the world for various reasons, if we want to try to understand what manifests itself as apathy or lack of commitment, we can remain open to the possibility of a form of mental rebellion such as the one Freud describes.

Despite Freud's theorization on this topic being full of contradictions and distinctions and so always open to revisions and changes, even when he uses enthusiastic or poetical tones, he always describes a nature that we must dominate. This can also be seen in the role he assigns to the death drive. In *Beyond the Pleasure Principle* (1920) Freud describes the death drive as a silent attraction, a tendency toward a mental state characterized by the absence of any tension, a mental state of indifference and inactivity. Because of their capacity to tend to previous states of mind and to alleviate the mind from its tension, the narcissistic satisfaction and the original masochism are expressions of man's aggressive and self-destructive drive.

> (...) But even where it emerges without any sexual purpose, in the blindest fury of destructiveness, we cannot fail to recognize that the satisfaction of the instinct is accompanied by an extraordinarily high degree of narcissistic enjoyment, owing to its presenting the ego with a fulfilment of the latter's old wishes for omnipotence. The instinct of destruction, moderated and tamed, and, as it were, inhibited in its aim, must, when

it is directed towards objects, provide the ego with the satisfaction of its vital needs and with control over nature.

(Freud, 1930, p. 121)

Knowledge of the good does not automatically determine the possibility that the good will be implemented.

In summary, Freud tries to simultaneously hold two apparently irreconcilable positions: love and respect for nature on the one hand and dominion over nature on the other.

A good relationship with nature in Freud's thought seems to be the other side of technical progress, its completion. This is a conflictual relationship, lacking full integration of polarities and contradictions: pain and happiness, play and seriousness, and individual need and social need.

It is no coincidence that Herbert Marcuse (1955) argued that the concept of man emerging from the Freudian theory is the most incontestable indictment of Western civilization and, at the same time, its most staunch defense.

However, already in the essay *The Uncanny* (1919) Freud proposed the dissolution of every form of "simple" imagination, of a comfortable dichotomous point of view. For him what is good and what is bad and what is familiar and what is not cannot be neatly characterized.

Ghosh (2016) reconsidered and updated some of Freud's reflections. He points that there is a further disorienting element in events caused by climate change. Although they are radically non-human, today's freakish weather events certainly are the sum of a number of human actions. Thus, the events provoked by global warming have a closer connection with humans than did the climatic phenomena of the past.

In *Civilization and Its Discontents*, Freud strongly criticized utopian socialists, who nostalgically propose *"(...) that we should be much happier if we gave it up and returned to primitive conditions"* (p. 86). Here emerged also a different point of view from that of Jung, who argued that the loss of feeling of a strong link with the material world mainly depended on the European scientific revolution of the 17th century.

Jung wrote (1962, p. 236):

We rush impetuously into novelty, driven by a mounting sense of insufficiency, dissatisfaction, and restlessness. We no longer live on what we have, but on promises, no longer in the light of the present day, but in the darkness of the future, which, we expect, will at last bring the proper sunrise. (...) Reforms by advances, that is, by new methods or gadgets, are of course impressive at first, but in the long they are dubious and in any case dearly paid for. They by no means increase the contentment or happiness of people on the whole. Mostly, they are deceptive sweetenings (sic) of existence, like speedier communication which unpleasantly accelerate the tempo of life and leave us with less time than ever before.

According to Jung (1962), from 1923 to 1956 (the year after his wife's death), he built the famous Bollingen Tower near Lake Zurich. Here, Jung, at almost 50, was not satisfied to give testimony to the psychoanalytic experience only through written and spoken words, so he embarked on the project of a house for summer holidays. At the beginning, it was only a circular building, a single tower, but then three new sections were added and the building was enlarged. For Jung, this enlargement indicated his psychical growth. When he was 80, Jung wanted to add a new floor to Bollingen Tower, a place without electricity or tap water and with a wood-burning stove, became a place for meditation, spiritual retreat and living testimony of the connection with nature.

In spite of the evident contradictions in Freud's thinking, his ideas and notes are important for a modern reflection on the issue of environmental responsibility. Nicola Emery (2011) positively comments on some of Freud's contributions: the ideas of sublimation, prudence, sharing, respect, taking care, management and responsibility. These are the virtues through which Western thought tried to do something with the use of technology. All these virtues express at different levels the need of a renunciation of instinct to direct technology in a sustainable manner.

A concern similar to that led Freud to theorize drive renunciation as the founding element of the construction of civilization can be found in Max Weber's philosophical thought. In *Politics as a Vocation*, the lecture he gave in Munich in 1919, a year before his death, Weber appeared disenchanted with the relationship between the "Ethic of Moral Conviction" (or "Ethic of Principles") (*Gesinnungsethik*) and "Ethic of Responsibility" (*Verantwortungsethik*). The former is an absolute ethics pertaining to those who act only by following those principles they deem right per se, regardless of consequences. The latter is the ethics of responsibility and refers to the presumed consequences of the choices and behaviors of an individual and his community. The ethics of moral conviction requires effort and means that an endeavor is not a static constitution and beauty or proportion of a certain form. They cannot be distinguished from the ethics of responsibility, which requires attention to the social meaning of an endeavor, the balanced management of space and their environmental sustainability. It is necessary, for example, to study the environmental impact of architectural works and construction or renovation technology that reduce pollution and energy consumption.

Freud was a man of his time. He could not consider the paradoxical and strong connection between the subjugation of nature to technology and pollution, that is, the universal production of every kind of garbage and dirt as that occurs these days (Emery, 2011). Of course, he lived in an era in which the optimistic growth of technical progress was exalted so that he could not warn us about the excess of technology that can destroy nature. In spite of this, at the beginning of *The Future of an Illusion* (1927a, p. 6), he has this intuition: *"Human creations are easily destroyed*, and the science and technology that have created them can also be used for their annihilation."

He also points out that (p. 53):

> We may insist as often as we like that man's intellect is powerless in comparison with his instinctual life, and we may be right in this. Nevertheless, there is something peculiar about this weakness. The voice of the intellect is a soft one, but it does not rest till it has gained a hearing. Finally, after a countless succession of rebuffs, it succeeds. This is one of the few points on which one may be optimistic about the future of mankind (…).

Notes

1 The theory of drive renunciation is opposed to what Karl Marx defends in his 1844 book, that is, that the sociality of workers cannot be instrumental to achieve a political goal. Rather, it is an immediate and "spontaneous" need. According to Marx, for workers, eating, smoking, and drinking together is the goal per se: socializing is the necessary condition, not the means, of any political project. Louis Althusser (1970) harkens back to Marxian intuitions and maintains that human beings have a certain experience of mastery over themselves. By referring to the relationship between the unconscious and ideology, he describes an experience subordinating the social drives to the rational and selfish desires of the individual. Ágnes Heller (1974) maintains that, before material needs, humans have radical needs (that she identifies with the social drives).
2 Some authors connect the Judeo-Christian tradition to ecological issues: Jay W. Forrester (1971) argues that Christianity is the religion of exponential economic growth; and Carl Amery (1972) argues that the maxim of Genesis 1.28 ["(…) have dominion over the fish of the sea and over the birds of the air and over every living thing that moves upon the Earth"] justifies the unstoppable dynamics of productivism.
3 Domenico Chianese (2015) reminds us of Darwin's fascinating story of the gardener bird that builds a nest by decorating it with pieces of cork, mirror insects, and orchid berries to court female birds. Then, he invites a female that, if she does not like the nest's architecture, can freely leave the nest. Here, we recognize an almost human sense of beauty to the female gardener bird.
4 Bion (1990, p. 100) focuses on the emotion that the primitive part of the mind registers upon confronting fundamental reality. He also stresses the risk of apathetic intellectualization emanating from the reductionism of scientism:

> (…) I would like to be capable of being awe-inspired by a sight like the aurora borealis. I would not think that I had improved if I said, 'Oh well, this is simply an electric display; it's an electric phenomenon.' That is clever, but not wise.

Chapter 4

Psychoanalysis and the environmental crisis

Although the first psychoanalysts, for example, Georg Groddeck (1923)[1] and Sándor Ferenczi (1924),[2] offer compelling reflections on the relationship between nature and humankind, it is in the 1960s that a more accurate analysis of it takes root.

In the years of atomic threat and fear of destruction of the planet, Harold F. Searles (1960) gives meaning to the "non-human" environment and everyday habitat. He expands the intuitions of Winnicott on the fusion between mother and child (the human environment) and the environment–individual setup. Searles refers to Winnicott's famous dictum (1960, p. 587, Note 1): *"There is no such thing as an infant meaning, of course, that whenever one finds an infant one finds maternal care, and without maternal care there would be no infant."* The things of the world have a psychic resonance and we cannot think of a child without his environment. In *Berlin Walls* (1969), Winnicott introduces another important topic, the far-reaching concept of environmental support and its effects on the development of a person. This support allows a person to "survive" primal fears of disintegration and hold together contradictory needs of being alone and being in relationship with others through construction of a True Self and improvement of the experience of being authentic.

René Spitz (1965) attributes the development of an affective deprivation disorder in children in orphanages exclusively to a lack of mothering. Searles (1960) takes it a step further: he hypothesizes that, in environments such as orphanages, the deprivation of non-human elements plays a crucial role. Unlike children in orphanages, those in nursery schools do not develop this deprivation disorder because they benefit from various sources of stimulation, for example, the presence of toys or the possibility of watching the world outside the window.

When it comes to mental growth – especially in childhood – plants, animals, architectural structures, and furniture play as important a role, as do the affective environment and the social milieu. Searles is 65 years old when he writes *The Nonhuman Environment in Normal Development and in*

DOI: 10.4324/9781003220077-5

Schizophrenia (1960). He remarks that he could have not written it when he was 40 years old and grappling with differentiating humans from nonhumans. Searles details a sense of conscious or unconscious relatedness between the individual and the non-human environment. This is an intimate affective relatedness between the processes of human life and those of the environment, a connection that we must respect and recognize for our mental well-being if we are to alleviate our existential solitude in the universe.

The benefits of this relatedness can be divided into four categories (Searles, 1960):

a   the alleviation of various painful and anxious emotional states
b   the promotion of self-realization
c   the strengthening of a personal feeling of reality
d   the fostering of appreciating and accepting other people.

According to Searles, the sense of relatedness weakens the fear of death and fosters a sense of peace, stability, continuity, and security. Finally, it can serve as an antidote against feelings of emptiness and insignificance.

Ecological deterioration causes anxieties (and their relative defenses) and thus leads to bias and an interruption of the sense of relatedness between human and non-human. Searles's 1972 paper about this topic is still relevant today. In this paper, he lays the dearth of psychoanalytic reflection of and contribution to the environmental crisis at the feet of unconscious destructive factors. He polemically argues that most psychoanalysts are so indifferent to and unaware of the environmental problem that they can diagnose in their colleagues interested in it psychotic depression or paranoid schizophrenia.

The generalized apathy about the ecological crisis is mainly based on the Ego's unconscious defenses against anxiety, according to Searles: our relationship with the environment comprises ambivalence and destructiveness and our Ego defenses swing between dependence and control, submission and exploitation, envy and gratitude. More precisely, these defenses involve:

–   The phallic and Oedipal phases of development. One of the main drivers behind fathers' apathy toward their sons being imperiled by extinction is the possibility that the crisis would vanquish an Oedipal rival, a feared, envied, hated, and never-defeated rival. Searles goes as far as to postulate an unconscious hatred toward future generations, our progeny, and their progeny in turn – vengeful fathers, determined to destroy birthright through neglect, bent on exacting revenge for the deprivations they suffered, in whatever development phase, at the hands of their own fathers. It is a hatred that includes and extends well beyond the Oedipal conflict.

– The early phases of development that more or less coincide with the Kleinian depressive position. Environmental pollution can hinder us from becoming aware of how deep a depression someone suffers. On top of feeling isolated in his depression, a person feels, along with everyone else, trapped in a ruined world. Pollution not only destroys the future of progeny that parents unconsciously hate and envy, it also denies a past that parents unconsciously resist remembering with great clarity. Parents equate the idealized world of their lost childhood with a pure environment. They erroneously assume that they cannot do anything about the climate crisis just as they cannot recover the world of their childhood and the feeling that they are retrospectively idealizing its deprived and painful features. The crisis allows parents to maintain the illusion of an ideal childhood, a non-contaminated childhood they can still obtain. In this sense, polluting parents unconsciously represent parts of their past to which they cling. These transference-distortions permeate their present environment and comfortably shield them from feeling the poignancy of past losses. Of course, we can only embrace and live in reality. Omnipotently, parents have destroyed the world in which their idealized childhood existed and they choose to increasingly degrade it by polluting it.

– The earlier phases more or less, coincide with the paranoid position. We can withstand a world so overwhelmingly ruled by technological, alien, complex, massive, and oppressive forces only through a regression to a state of non-differentiation from it. We experience our increasingly polluted world as an omnipresent enemy. This paralyzes us into terror-induced inactivity. We live in a deeply regressed form of experience, in which we are non-differentiated from our environment. We do not possess a clearly separate self that allows us to face the "outer" threat. At this level of primitive Ego functioning, we cannot differentiate between a good and a bad mother. Too often nature has been a bad mother to us, whereas technology has been a good one because it allows us to control nature. Now our good mother is poisoning us and if we do not curb her and return nature to its unfettered condition, we risk getting lost. We praise technology: the annual gross national product epitomizes its growth. We consider technology a kind of God. Now we are supposed to renounce this God to save ourselves.

Searles's 1972 paper concludes with humankind's current dilemma: to save the real world or to use it as an instrument of destruction against us all? Our greatest danger is neither the hydrogen bomb nor the more slowly lethal effects of pollution emanating from technology: it is that the state of the world evokes our earliest anxieties and, simultaneously, offers us the delusional and deadly "promise" to manage these anxieties, to efface them, by externalizing and giving flesh and blood to those primitive conflicts that cause those anxieties. The greatest danger we face, what can lead to our extinction, is our belief that we are omnipotently free of human conflict.

The American psychoanalyst extends his psychoanalytic comprehension from the most common understanding of "environment" – the biosphere – to all conditions influencing life, reproduction, and human development: for Searles, the environment is not limited to a past inscribed inside of us and occurring around us, it also encompasses a future that is to come, the future of those generations who will dearly pay the consequences of our relationship with the biosphere (Magnenat, 2019c).

Psychoanalytic reflections of the 2000s

After too long a silence, rarely interrupted by the occasional isolated voice, in the 2000s, psychoanalysts recommence to reflect on the relationship between humans and the environment. We will see throughout this book that they begin from Searles's considerations and his reflections on the theories of Freud, Klein, and Winnicott.

Among the earlier, infrequent voices, we find Ezio Cirincione with his 1991 *Ecologia e Psicoanalisi* (Ecology and Psychoanalysis). With passion and worry, the book is a forerunner, because it deals with a new topic for the psychoanalysis of its time: how human destruction poses a mortal attack on the entire ecosystem, humankind included. Cirincione dramatically labels "delirium of denial," an irrational neo-construction of reality, the collusive indifference with which the environmental crisis is belittled. If a classic delirium of psychotic or depressive patients is that of the end of the world, in these times, the most dangerous and socially widespread delusional condition is its opposite: that is to believe it is impossible to destroy the world and that life on Earth will continue eternally. An example is the feverish delusional idealization of the creativity of technology in spite of human-created disasters and their ceaseless threats.

In her review of Cirincione's book, Franca Meotti (1992) agrees that human myopia endangers the ecosystem, but she does not share his catastrophic outlook. She offers a wide and less dramatic perspective about aggression, one that envisions not only envious destruction but also a peculiar relationship with beauty. Since pre-historic times, humans have damaged or killed the most beautiful of creatures and transformed them into animal trophies. Today, we have the sad privilege of witnessing an increasing number of such actions due to life conditions on the planet. At the same time, we have at our disposal psychoanalytic methods of inquiry that we can use to save ourselves and to reject another form of denial – the denial of possessing recourse or, at least, an ability to fight off self-illusion.

Technology is not a problem per se: the problem is that technological research is guided by the interests of international corporations and not by the aim to improve living conditions. Technology can be gravely problematic when, in a frenzied manner, we use it to deny our emotions, affects, internal and external objects, and the unconscious itself. For Magnenat (2019c), the unconscious is a terrorist, an undesirable who cannot stop returning, both individually and collectively, in a world we would like to be more civilized. Technology, at the industrial, information, genetic, and artificial intelligence level, can obscure our thoughts and dehumanize us, especially when it aligns with our human need to control our unconscious, rendering us slaves.

Lorena Preta (2019a) revisits Searles's topics, stressing that humanity is mainly a construct, a peculiar feature that is innately bestowed upon us at the beginning but that needs to interact with an environment to develop and distinguish from the natural world as well as the artificial one – two worlds that will always be part of our humanity. Both the notion of humanity and our experience of belonging to humanity require extended space in which the subject can assume others' alterities. This does not necessarily mean that the subject is absorbed in this space and thus becomes indistinct from it: the subject must continually adjust to expansion or increase.

For Roberto Esposito (2016), the inside–outside relationship ought to be interpreted in three ways: first, as a hyper-immunization that raises barriers and makes our identity harsher; next, as a complete lack of immunization that abolishes all borders and makes us lose our identity. Neither hyper-immunization nor lack of immunization can be accepted because they destroy the organism: in the former, identity is suppressed; in the latter, it becomes so open as to dissolve. The third manner, immunization through contamination, enriches and strengthens our identity. This form of immunization follows the logic of inclusion–exclusion: for Esposito, this must be intended as a bio-logic because it is ontologically founded in the functioning of the immune system.

Laura Ambrosiano (2017) reconsiders the reflections of Derrida, Foucault, and Esposito. The inside–outside overlap makes us conceive our psychic apparatus and its functioning as contaminated from the beginning. It is as if we carry an alien inside of us, something that severely restricts our common illusion of becoming subjects. Instead of an opposition between the internal and external worlds, we think of an outside–inside or an inside–outside[3] that stresses the limits of becoming a subject and endorses the idea of an extended mind.

Chinese thinking is cyclical and different from Western thought in which linearity is the basis of current technological growth. Where Western thought values the individual, Confucian and Taoist thinking is rooted in a millennial tradition and places the human being at the center of societies and the world. In the Confucian Rén 人 (human being or person), the supreme virtue is the feeling of humanity, for we become human only in relationship with others. Westerners tend to be so immersed in technological omnipotence that they are unable to question globalization based on unlimited greed and quick profit in spite of the ethical conditions at the basis of the social and in the face of a planet that is devastated by our choices. There is the connection between psychoanalysis and Ancient Chinese thinking: both value and put at their center the human dimension (Lauret, 2020).

According to the Indian psychoanalyst Sudhir Kakar (1997), unlike its Western counterpart, Indian culture conceives the body as an interconnected one with nature and the cosmos, in a continuous eco-systemic exchange between humans and the environment. Hinduism, particularly, its doctrine of reincarnation considers the human being as a transitional step toward varied forms of life and thus advocates respect for all species. By contrast, according to the Western image of the body, the natural features of the environment – healthy air quality, plentiful sunlight, and thriving flora and fauna – are a priori irrelevant to emotional and cognitive growth.

But Hinduism maintains the concept of the individual. It believes in the *Brahma* as a universal soul, but assumes that this soul exists in each person in a peculiar manner: the Self or *Atman.* For Hinduism, there is a strong connection between *dharma* (the ethical, social, and divine order of things) and *karma* (personal actions) (Bollas, 2012).

The desert, the mountain, the sea, the forest, and, above all, the animals have certainly an extraordinary capacity to help in supporting specific symptoms, particularly those related to phobias. Although the landscape and the animals can provide material for both symptoms and dreams, we should not reduce them simply in such a function of providing symbolic material for our mind. Ethological studies demonstrate that we cannot deny elements of external natural forms of sensibility and language anymore (Demailly, 2020).

Antonio Prete begins his book *Il Cielo Nascosto* (the Hidden Sky) (2016) with Martin Buber's statement as exergue: "If Thou is said, the I of the combination I-Thou is said along with it." Here, "thou" is not only the other human being because the other can also assume the form of other natural things such as other living beings, land, seas, stars, and galaxies.

Chianese (2018) finds in Prete's considerations the value of a meditation on the living being, on all living beings, and on the relationship between the human being and the living being surrounding and moving him or her. In these terms, he finds a connection between Prete's thought and psychoanalytic theories.

This endless work of adjustment is onerous. Perhaps this difficulty constitutes one of the primary unconscious hindrances in tending to our planet. We unconsciously identify with technology, which we perceive as omnipotent and immortal, so as to avoid seeing the dark side of our social well-being and of the Western way of living, in spite of the copious amount of information about the condition of our planet.

Sennett (2018) believes that if Heidegger were alive today and could observe human-made climate disasters, he undoubtedly would say, "I told you so!" and "You had the wrong idea about nature, you thought you could bend it to your will."

In his *Symposium* (385–370 BC), Plato writes that Eros is the son of Penia (poverty) and Poros (abundance). One of the contemporary challenges lies in finding a balance between overabundance and dearth: we must scale down the former to face the latter. It follows that we tend to protect ourselves from intolerable feelings of insignificance, deprivation, loss, fear of death, and that sense of guilt and shame that result from our implicit complicity with something inhuman, something that constitutes the annihilation of what is human (Fédida et al., 2007), as we blindingly exploit natural resources, never mind the cost and destructive consequences. Our reaction to all of this is a mere pervasive apathy that takes the forms of indifference, disregard, negligence, greed, inattention, laziness, and understatement.

These considerations are found in a nutshell in *Formulations on the Two Principles of Mental Functioning* (1911). Here, Freud defines the baby "his majesty" because it considers the maternal disposition to satisfy its urgent needs limitless and perpetually guaranteed. So, too, Klein (1935) describes a child who unconsciously fantasizes about the inexhaustibility of the maternal breast, which he wants to totally possess, as he wants to possess the mother's whole body.

Sally Weintrobe (2013a) suggests that when we confront the climate emergency, we must tackle three different forms of denial: denialism, negation, and disavowal. Each of the three has radically varied effects:

1   We can easily recognize denialism because it involves the intentional broadcasting of fake news about climate change for commercial, political, and ideological aims. We find a cynical and planned defensive modality in political campaigns and product advertisements. It minimizes the extent of the collateral damage caused by the environmental impact or contests the value of scientific discovery. A recipe for disaster is the combination of defenses at the individual level[4] and political denial organized by lobbies that perversely promote consumerism and the colonization of the biosphere for mere economic interest.

2   Negation is exemplified by the statement that something does not exist when it actually does exist. This defense allows us to grapple with anxiety and loss. It is a form of denial characterized first by a phase of mourning, in which a person begins to accept a seemingly intolerable reality. The individual opposes reality but does not distort it. He may start by saying, "It is not true," then, with irritation, accept that it is true, and, finally, transition to experience grief and acceptance. It is also possible to use negation not as a flexible stage of mourning but in a clearly psychotic manner.

3   Disavowal is a more problematic defense because it implies simultaneously knowing and not knowing. On the one hand, we know and accept reality but, on the other, through a sort of psychological alchemy, we staunchly minimize its meaning. It is like having one eye open and

another closed. Throughout time, this defensive modality has been especially dangerous and difficult to treat because our defenses tend to be more rigid and rooted according to the increase in our anxieties. It is as if we put ourselves in an alternate reality to control the increasing negative emotions: we unconsciously and perversely attack rational and logical meaning, and as an alternative, we propose a sort of anti-meaning. Disavowal functions via constant monitoring of the feelings of annoyance provoked by violence and the relative suffering related to the difficult historical moments we experience. This monitoring prevents us from confronting the turmoil we experience, but it helps us tap into reparative psychological modalities to detach from it.

Irma Brenman Pick (2013) points out that a human being exhibits toward Mother Nature[5] the same fantasies of possession that a child exhibits toward the mother. In fact, the human being simultaneously wants the advantages and comforts of industrialization and an idyllically uncontaminated world, without any renunciation. It is as when some analysands say, "Please, God, make me virtuous, but not now."

It is burdensome to renounce the status quo, to rationally accept reality and, at the same time, to deny reality. There is a glaring disjunction between taking a rational position and rejecting the consequences of such a position in terms of lifestyle changes, production means, and consumer habits. For example, many people recognize global warming as a problem but do not situate it in current reality. They conveniently contextualize it in a more or less hypothetical future, a possible problem for their children and grandchildren that can be avoided for the moment or repaired.

Rosemary Randall (2009) explores the possible regression to the early state of splitting, where what is good and what is bad is clearly distinct, as a powerful psychological defense against climate crisis. She argues that this produces a world of extremes, in which the good is idealized and the bad is conceived as a monster. The fear of loss leads to split off and project the effects of climate change onto the future. The present continues to appear safe, but at the expense of a terrifying future. On the one hand, we have a nightmare, on the other, a false comfort.

Apathy allows us to de-problematize our fears and stress the length of time before we fully experience the consequences of global warming. It also makes it easier for us to skeptically question the credibility and authority of science (Hamilton, 2013).

Another perversely defensive modality is to consider individual pleasure and the advantages of the present – despite the vast disadvantages heaped on others and the environment – a universal pleasure through confounding ways that distort reality (Hoggett, 2013).

Yuval Noah Harari concludes his book *Sapiens* (2011) arguing that we are self-made gods with the law of physics to keep us company: we are accountable to no one. As a consequence, we are provoking the destruction of our fellow animals and of the surrounding ecosystem. This is because we consider only our own comfort and amusement, yet never finding satisfaction. Finally, Harari asks whether there is anything more dangerous than dissatisfied and irresponsible self-made gods who are not aware of what they want.

Because it is too difficult to get in touch with our deepest anxieties, we rid ourselves of every sense of responsibility and awareness of having a role in the creation of this damage. We assume an exasperated form of justification according to which we pass from "It is the same, everyone does it!" to "It is the same, everyone likes it!"

In a sense, this is akin to the pedophile; for him or her the child is a willing partner and thus symmetrically co-responsible; sexual desire is reciprocal and the child shares his or her pleasure. The pedophile believes that the child wants the same things he or she wants. He or she neither recognizes nor respects the child's emotional consistency: he or she thinks, desires, and construes the child as a sort of homunculus, an artificial small adult who, once reified, exactly matches the pedophile's excited construction (Schinaia, 2001).

John Keene (2013) refers to Winnicott's thought (1965) and points out that we experience the Earth as a limitless "toilet-mother," an enormous dump absorbing our toxicity endlessly, just as we discharge our sewage into the sea. So painful and hateful are the child's dependency needs that they can lead to a wish for punishment, control, or destruction of the mother, who is felt as the main source of the child's frustrations. Furthermore, the pleasure of destruction brings a quicker and more immediate satisfaction than the painful and difficult process of creation and repair.

In *The Psycho-Analytical Process* (1967) Donald Meltzer develops the concept of "toilet-breast," stressing how, at the psychological level, the breast is not only something nourishing but also something in which we evacuate our intolerable states of mind.

In his *Psychoanalysis and Ecology at the Edge of Chaos* (2011), Joseph Dodds considers some different psychoanalytic paradigms and the theories of Felix Guattari, who refutes the dualistic opposition between the human system (culture) and the non-human system (nature). Dodds argues for the presence of a series of non-linear, non-predictable, and highly complex interconnected systems that come into play in the phenomena of climate change and that provokes fears and anxieties in individuals, groups, and communities at the national and international levels. This determines those interconnections between the local and the interplanetary ecology that a single discipline cannot comprehend. According to Dodds, psychoanalysis can play an important role as part of a wider ecology of ideas. To do this, we must develop a meta-perspective or meta-theory that can integrate the many disparate strands (disparate in terms of our arbitrary divisions, not in terms of how the world really is). Dodds proposes that we connect the psychoanalytic approach with non-linear and ecological thought to unify the "three ecologies" – mind, nature, and society – and to answer the thorny question of why humans do not take critical action to efficaciously respond to climate emergency, in spite of contemporary science's almost complete knowledge of its catastrophic aspects. The defense mechanisms and intra-psychical tactics we use to control our overwhelming anxiety about the ecological disaster hinder us from constructing efficacious repairing responses. They include splitting, intellectualization, repression, displacement, suppression, and denial. The question is whether the central dynamic consists of a growing anxiety as a response to an enormous problem, whose magnitude is so great that we need a defense, or whether our anxiety increases because the great abstractness of the problem makes it difficult to comprehend on the basis of human emotions. For Dodds, it is plausible that these two factors work together. He refers to Melanie Klein's developmental phases when he writes about the fantasy of an "Earth-breast" infinitely at our disposal, the schizo-paranoid response to the necessary weaning and the need to move toward the depressive position, characterized by the desire to repair loss, pain, and frustration.

Also J.-P. Matot (2020) refers to an intersection between psychoanalysis and complex systems. He proposes the concept of dispersed Self, which can be conceived in a theory of the Self wider than that of the Self localized in a bodily shell and thus including a multiplicity of shells.

Alan Bellamy (2019) focuses on another defense against the awareness of the seriousness of climate crisis by renewing Ferenczi's concept of identification with the aggressor, according to which through identification or introjection, the aggressor disappears as an external reality (Ferenczi, 1932). Bellamy exhorts us to apply this concept not only to cases of child sexual abuse, but also to situations of traumatic imbalance between the individual and his environment, when fear becomes so unbearable that the individual feels himself to be in inescapable danger and experiences a lack of protection from the surrounding world. Our response extends beyond dissociation and, to protect ourselves, becomes an identification with the surrounding world, with the very thing we fear. Here Bellamy reconsiders Searles, according to whom, under such conditions, the individual gives in to secret fantasies of omnipotent destructiveness, to identify with the forces that threaten to destroy the world.

A further defensive modality is rationalization or intellectualization, in which rational comprehension of the gravity of the environmental crisis does not match emotional comprehension. Knowledge that is unable to trigger a consequent action is particular to this moment in history (Cohen, 2000).

For Foer (2019), the distance between awareness and feeling can make it impossibly difficult to act, even for people who are thoughtful and politically active: it is that exhausting to ponder the complexity of the threats we must face.

On the one hand, we are emotionally alerted and scared from the growing loss of biodiversity and the intensity of climate changes but, on the other hand, we seem to be unable to consider these alerts and our daily routines and to connect global and distant events and data and the urgency of change in the local dimension (Van Aken, 2020). Otherwise, we can also find opposing defensive modalities in which feelings and ineffability are more valorized than thinking and cognitive comprehension. These defensive modalities are typical of a romantic, Edenic, and sublime vision according to which nature must always be protected and maintained untouched and immutable over time.

It is plausible that cavemen would have been able to survive under these conditions as long as they would have immediately responded to an acutely felt fear, such as confronting a predator or enemy. Rather, if fear would have been expanded and slowly developed, even if it would have been determined by a potentially dangerous situation, it would have been much easier to ignore (Keene, 2013). Unfortunately, human beings and societies do not have the gift of foresight, so tend to react only to present situations.

We are better when we confront a clear and present danger, a peril we can see, hear, sniff, and smell, a hazard characterized by linear causality, an easily identifiable enemy who poses direct personal consequences. Instead, we remove from the heart what is invisible, especially if it is uncomfortable.

We experience distant objects, as if they were in the shadows, in some forgotten place, in a land existing in a distant and unimaginable future. Environmental issues are considered as distant, as something specialized that must be treated only by few experts. The unconscious aim of this mental operation is the creation of an emotional distance from those things we feel guilty for mistreating (Weintrobe, 2013b).

Umberto Galimberti (2019) argues that when misfortune befalls a close beloved relative, we suffer with him and try to help, as if the misfortune befell us. When it is a neighbor, we feel sorry for them and offer comforting words. When a tragedy occurs far from us – say, a genocide in the heart of Africa or a tsunami in the Middle East – we consider it merely as news. Our mind connects to events in the surrounding world (in German, Umwelt) but not to those in the world in general (Welt).

Andri Snær Magnason (2019) argues that it is easier to form an opinion on minor issues, for example, when someone breaks an object worth millions, when someone shoots an animal, or when an initiative turns out to be too expensive. But when we come to something infinitely great or sacred, even to the foundation of our existence, we do not have a proportionate reaction. It is as if the brain cannot assess the sizes.

In his novel *The Plague* (1947), Albert Camus argues that human beings are utterly unable to share in suffering what they cannot see when they are too remote.

We continue to breathe, to drink water, to swim in the sea, to play in the snow, and to enjoy green spaces without any concrete sensation of danger. We tend to propose simplified narratives and interpretations. Complex problems, which we cannot immediately see, demonstrate our impotence. We tend to defend from this impotence by trivializing those cognitive dissonances that foment our lack of interest, our spacing dynamics, or even our mental dullness. We feel forced to limit our mind, activate a system of anti-knowledge, live as amorphous spectators without responsibility rather than intrinsically co-responsible actors. It is arduous to accept our co-participation to so enormous a crime.

Meltzer (1986, pp. 189–190) wrote:

> Although the magnitude of the threats that this planet and its population face seems to have escalated beyond anything previously known, it is perhaps not always useful to approach the problems facing mankind from this quantitative vertex. The difficulty lies in-+ our limited capacity for thought and its foundation in adequate emotional responsiveness. It may seem, superficially, that cataclysm stirs us deeply but careful examination suggests something quite contrary. (…) The 'end of the world' can be stated in megatons rather than, as by Laputa's astronomical mathematicians, in terms of the temperature of the tail of the comet – or, in the language of the Old Testament prophet, as God's wrath, but this does not make the concept any more stirring of emotion. For horror is a perverse state of excitement (…).

The undue influence of post-modern culture is at play here, according to Kaës (2013): we live in constant urgency because our temporal horizon has been reduced by cultural components such as hyper-control, undifferentiation, omnipotence, and the fascination for the extreme. Immediacy has transformed our notion of time. Our relationship with time values the synchronous encounter, what is here and now. Short time prevails over long time, zapping and nomadism over continuity. The link is maintained only in the present moment. It escapes history because the only certainty is that the future is undecided.

Heinz Kohut (1981) proposes the notion of the cultural self-object, a psychical figure permitting human groups and culture to recognize themselves when they construe their identity as a group self and thus acquire a relative sense of continuity and cohesion in sharing a common ideal. Following Kohut's notion, Alfredo Lombardozzi (2020) develops the notion of the cultural/environmental self-object, a form of relationship with the natural forms that are not conceived only as stranger than or different from ours, but as pertaining to the dynamic articulation of the deep connection between nature and culture.

A psychoanalytic interpretation of the difficulties of the human being–environment relationship, an interpretation that can be made on very different theoretical models, can help assess the unconscious dynamics and the complex ways of relationships. In fact, this assessment can contrast the tendency to construe highly sophisticated forms of denial and foster a new relationship between nature and culture, a relationship neither dichotomous nor excessively and improperly based on assimilation.

Notes

1 In *The Book of the It* (1923) Groddeck argues that the language of the It (the term he uses to designate the Unconscious) is the language of the world. Thus, he opposes the distinction between the organic and the psychic.
2 Freud (1933, p. 228) appreciates Ferenczi's *Thalassa: A Theory of Genitality* (1924):

> This little book is a biological rather than a psycho-analytic study; it is an application of the attitudes and insights associated with psycho-analysis to the biology of the sexual processes and, beyond them, to organic life in general. It was perhaps the boldest application of psycho-analysis that was ever attempted.

3 Derrida (1976) appeals to an inside dug from the outside, of an outside hollowed out from the inside. Foucault (1966) refers to "the thought of the outside," thoughts preceding subjects (thoughts without thinkers?). He criticizes the notion of a subject who stays inside and owns the meaning of his own words. The meaning of words emanates from the outside world, which permeates and enfolds the subject: it inhabits the subject and defines his limits.
4 These defenses are part of human nature and the result of millennia in the history of civilization. They result in a limited and circumscribed responsibility.
5 In her novel, *The Fifth Season* (2015), the writer Nora K. Jemisin does not talk of Mother Earth but of Father Earth to stress that Earth does not give us love but rules to follow. If we do not respect them, we can expect a violent reaction.

Chapter 5

Waste[1]

Jean Baudrillard (1978) argues that psychoanalysis is the first great theory about residuals (such as dreams and slips) because it is based on the recovery of fragments of memory.

In *Three Essays on the Theory of Sexuality* (1905), Freud focuses on the pleasure that comes from evacuating the feces during the anal-sadistic stage of psychosexual development. Between 18 and 36 months, the child derives satisfaction by controlling the anal sphincter. Controlling and expelling bodily products are not only a form of gratification for the child but also a tool for regulating the relationships with his environment. Evacuating feces goes along with the fear of loss and the feeling of incompleteness, which in turn can provoke obsessive control related to holding in the feces. The decision to urinate or defecate is the first symbolic act of denial or appeasement of the need for self-control imposed by parental figures and, by extension, social institutions. Thus, it is the first moment in which an individual submits to a set of shared social norms. Thanks to the increased ability to control the sphincter, the pleasure derived from evacuating (anal eroticism) leads to libido gratification and the emergence of an aggressive character (the anal-sadistic phase). In the same manner, the development of self-esteem and autonomy are associated with the development of the ability to voluntarily control defecation. The inability to deal with conflicts and incorrect toilet training at this stage can lead to developing an anal fixation (retentive or expulsive). The expulsive anal fixation originates from excessive gratification in the anal-sadistic phase and from an excessively permissive education. It manifests itself in the child's tendency to defecate in inappropriate places and can lead to an expulsive anal trait, which in turn leads to an extremely disorganized personality, cruel and destructive, with a tendency toward manipulation. In cases of unsatisfactory gratification, the child derives from retaining the feces in spite of the education imparted by the parents, causing a retentive anal fixation. The future anal retentive adult will be characterized by extreme attention to detail and a great sense of possession, be parsimonious, well organized, obstinate, and obsessed by order and hygiene. These two types of characters favor different emotional and

DOI: 10.4324/9781003220077-6

cultural attitudes in the production and collection of waste, with disordered dissipation or, conversely, obsessive control.[2]

The return of the repressed, as described by Freud in *Delusion and Dream in Jensen's Gradiva* (1907), is the process according to which the repressed elements, which repression never destroys, tend to reappear in consciousness through the same associative mechanisms that were used to repress them. The return of the repressed leads us to deal with our "dirt," with our internal waste, our aspects that we feel ethically and socially unbecoming and from which we defend ourselves, as we defend ourselves from waste representing the hidden shadow of our culture.

Yet, in Freud's conception in *The Uncanny* (1919) that unwelcome residue of the mind, that object we try to repress, remains mysteriously familiar and resists every attempt at separation and does not constitute anything new or foreign. And so, waste, with its potentially damaging effects, reminds us of our fragile and transitory nature.

The Break of Dawn, known as the "garbage barge," and its tugboat represent the return of the repressed. The barge and the tugboat sailed on March 22, 1987 from Islip, a town in New York's Long Island, in search of a landfill willing to welcome them. The 10,000 kilometers of travel up and down the Atlantic Coast was worthless: in fact, the trash was rejected by five U.S. states and three foreign states (North Carolina, Louisiana, Alabama, Mississippi, and Florida and Mexico, Belize, and the Bahamas). The garbage returned, after about four months, on May 16, to New York, where it remained anchored off the port of Long Island City waiting for the authorities to agree on its final destination. According to a plan that was subsequently prepared, the now-putrid waste was burned in a Brooklyn incinerator during a ten-day operation that produced about 400 tons of ash that were buried in Islip, where the whole story started.

For Lynch (1990), the residual, the decline, and the death in our mind are related. According to him, dissipation and loss are the dark side of change and indicate the existence of a pornography of the residual, similar to the pornography of sex and death. The accumulation of solid waste and the ever-growing contamination of air and water worry us. We cannot easily dispose of any: our old poisons return to us.

Waste is an inevitable part of our being in the world, our metaphorical counterpart, and therefore it reminds us harshly of what we really are and will become. Perhaps this is an invitation to reflect and rethink more on our connection with death than with that life that we would like to live longer and longer, continuing to deepen and reuse our knowledge of the world, a knowledge which today destroys the environment that sustains us (Scanlan, 2005).

Freud showed concern for environmental degradation, and attention to the care and disposal of waste and the effects of chemical and heat emissions from large urban centres. He was probably influenced by the conceptualisations of one of the pioneers of ecological research, his English patient in the years 1922–23, Arthur Tansley, who coined the term "ecosystem" to recognize the integration of the biotic community and its physical environment as a fundamental unit of ecology, within a hierarchy of physical systems that span the range from atom to universe.

In "The Ego and the Id" (1923, pp. 56–57) Freud writes:

> But since the ego's work of sublimation results in a defusion of the instincts and a liberation of the aggressive instincts in the super-ego, its struggle against the libido exposes it to the danger of maltreatment and death. In suffering under the attacks of the super-ego or perhaps even succumbing to them, the ego is meeting with a fate like that of Protista which are destroyed by the products of decomposition that they themselves have created, From the economic point of view the morality that functions in the super-ego seems to be a similar product of decomposition.

Waste is the other side of consumerist cultures, in which the goods are the objects of desire and pleasure in the present. We tend to hide waste for not discussing our idea of nature as distant and socially controlled.

Many climate-change skeptics have a maliciously perverted attitude about the amount of waste that they produce, as if producing a lot of waste was a reason for not believing or considering these issues. For these skeptics, evacuating is a pleasure but a shameful pleasure that we must enjoy in private and never name.

Among all living creatures, human beings are those producing the most waste. They are innocent victims used in a noble or ignoble way. Everything seems to converge toward a state of waste to the point where we are literally surrounded by it: debris of old satellites and other devices orbit the space above Earth.

Calvino (1972) describes the city of Leonia, whose citizens throw away old things and substitute them with new ones every single day. The consequence of this behavior is the production of a mountain of waste that risks overtaking the city. He writes that on the sidewalks, encased in spotless plastic bags, the remains of yesterday's Leonia await the garbage truck. There are not only squeezed tubes of toothpaste, blown-out light bulbs, newspapers, containers, wrappings, but also boilers, encyclopedias, pianos, and porcelain dinner services.

Managing our waste, especially toxic waste, affects deeply everything about us, from our feelings to our health to our daily life, it makes us question our very survival. We cannot ignore our waste anymore, we cannot send it to a Third World country or bury it in deep and remote places, because it comes back to torment us. Consider, for example, the creation of illegal landfills in our own backyards, poisoning the very environment in which the criminals constructing these dumps live with their families. Marco Sarno (2016) refers to crimes against Mother Earth, with a parallel destruction of the internal and external environment. Mother Earth being raped in the name of greed finds its roots in the Mafia and ignorance. An example of this is what happened in the so-called land of fires.[3] The waste fraudulently disposed with illegal methods emerges again in terms of decay and disease precisely through the burnings of waste and their toxic releases.

Paul Hoggett (2013) points out that greed has started to have a positive, not a negative, value. Having what we want and possessing it, fills an internal void that is not filled by love, comprehension, or personal growth. He laments the decline of every type of authority that could limit our desires of omnipotence.

Luckily, in recent years, we are beginning to see promising examples of landscape recovery of areas used as landfills. One example is the Vall d'en Joan landfill inside the Garraf Natural Park in Spain. In 1974, it began to be used as a dump for most of the waste from the Barcelona metropolitan area. Thanks to a complex multidisciplinary intervention that started in 2002, the area has been transformed into a large public park with cultivated terraces, wooded areas, agriculture fields, and nature trails.

Clinical vignette – Loredana: the filthy biologist

Loredana, a 32-year-old biologist, begins an analysis due to her tendency to break her romantic relationships with men when they make sexual advances. After some months in which she speaks mainly of her disgust for men "who only think only about that" and which she always refuses, she brings to the session a vague and confused memory from childhood. She was eight years old and lived with her parents in a small village in Calabria, a region in Southern Italy. Her mother sent her to buy bread from the baker:

> It is possible that, after having given me a sweet, the baker pulled down my panties and touched my privates. I went back home completely shocked and I told my mummy everything. But my mummy did not believe me, she said that nothing happened, that I invented everything and that I didn't have to think about it anymore. Nonetheless, from that day my parents did not send me to the baker anymore. I'm not able to say if this story is true, I mean, if it was real or invented, as my mother said. My problem is not known what really happened.

To protect her from reliving the trauma of seduction, the mother subjected her to the trauma of removing the meaning of reality. Because she was not inclined to accept her confused tension, she impeded to her any process of working through.

One of Loredana's most evident symptoms is her difficulty to sort waste and put it in appropriate bins. Although she is a biologist and rationally and scientifically convinced of the ecological value of recycling, when she must deal with waste, she is unable to make a symbolic investment, representing the useful transformation of the waste. She even justifies her behavior by defining it as anti-ideological and in opposition to the ecological ambitions of fashionable behaviors not based on scientific knowledge.

Only when the more confused and blamed aspects of her memory of the baker's seduction begin to unravel does she start to be able to distinguish the bad from the good in her mind. This marks the beginning of a possible symbolic transformation of garbage as something useful and new through recycling. When she begins to reduce the confusion and to separate the good and caring mother from the bad mother, who was unable to listen to her traumatic story and to tolerate her tormented truth and not pass it off as childish fantasy, Loredana stops being a little filthy criminal and begins to recycle and thus to separate the paper, plastic, metal, and glass, allowing a transformation inside and outside, which opens new spaces in her mental life and favors a new possibility of reusing what happened, of repairing as well as using the world (Lynch, 1990). She can find new transformative possibilities for the things she destructively threw away in a confused albeit ideologically justified way.

Clinical vignette – Antonio: the hyper-recycling surgeon

Antonio is a plastic surgeon known for being precise and able to control every stage of surgery in the operating room. Not only does he scrupulously control his own gestures and maneuvers, but he also exerts strict control over every single member of his team, even when he does not directly operate. He asks me for a consultation because he cannot explain why his hand has started to tremble and hesitate in the operating room, no longer as firm and decisive as the hand of a good surgeon should be. He feels inside himself a worry, even a sense of terror, that he might hurt his patients. At home, he is so meticulous in sorting waste that he seems fanatic. His has an evidently obsessive rite: putting in order what ends up in the unsorted waste container. Antonio demands that his wife and sons participate in this rite and harshly blames them for the slightest mistake. He has many containers than those normally supplied to families. Further, they are numbered and are of different colors. For Antonio, waste-sorting must be done not merely based on the type of waste[4] but also on the dimension of a single waste. At home, Antonio behaves like a policeman who must control the traffic of waste. Over time, this becomes his main activity when he is not at work.[5] When Antonio starts to feel his hands tremble in the operating room, he begins to attenuate and then lose his rigid and sacred control over waste. What his family initially hails as a miracle, the end of Antonio's vexations, becomes a matter of worry because Antonio's attitude and behavior radically change and no one can understand why. Without his ritual clothes, he throws rubbish in the street,[6] he is no longer interested in his perfectionistic waste-sorting, and he seems increasingly apathetic and indifferent. The crisis with the appearance of tremors in the operating room and his fear of unwillingly hurting his patients seems to be connected to Antonio's unexpected feelings about his personal life. Until then, Antonio repressed these feelings from his mental space and concretely and neatly identified with something that he could separate and expel in various recycling containers. The appearance of these unexpected feelings subverts his existence of security and routine, a safe and repetitive existence based on strong splitting. The event provoking these feelings is a sexual relationship with a young operating room assistant. Until that moment, Antonio has been able to manage this relationship in a clandestine and complementary way with his stable but sentimentally and sexually impoverished marital relationship. The transformation from a clandestine and rigorously controlled sexual relationship to a deeply involved intimate relationship puts an end to a life regulated with chronometric precision. Gone is the border distinguishing order and disorder. Antonio feels insecure and helpless; he cannot even count on his rigid splitting. The situation undermines his professional skills, as well as his strongly controlled and meticulous waste-sorting. In this case, the passage from separated to unseparated waste and the tremors in the operating room are signals of a crisis in personal identity, an identity that risks losing its boundaries and suffers from a feeling of an imminent catastrophe. In the analytic relationship, Antonio and I worked on considering these unexpected feelings as lifeblood, as the appearance of existential features mitigating the great economic effort required by perfect control. We considered that these feelings must not be seen as necessarily destructive. This work permitted Antonio to get in contact with the fear, the dirt, the disorder, the conflict between security and passion, to feel himself "more human" and not "a machine," without having to build exhausting and highly complex obsessive rites, but to accept limitations and compassion.

Clinical vignette – Bruna: the consumerist teacher

Bruna is 36 years old and teaches history and philosophy at a prestigious classical high school in the city. When she comes to her first session, she is overweight and wears scruffy clothes. The lack of care for her person contrasts with her elegant and fluid speech, a speech that is sometimes refined, and with her high cultural background.

She says she is the second child of a wealthy couple who married quite late, when they were both around 40. When he was eight months old, the firstborn, her brother Bruno, died of diphtheria. Exactly a year after his death, she was born. Her parents gave her the same name of her dead brother and did not have any other children. They were hyper-protective, feared she might die, too, and attributed to her those physical, spiritual, and intellectual features that they would have desired for the dead sibling, making her a revenant[7] of the dead son (Kestenberg, 1989; Jucovy, 1992). They covered her up more than necessary and kept her at home as much as possible so that she would not get sick. The excess of warm clothes substituted the emotional warmth her parents dedicated to the memory of the dead brother.

She had only to study and eat a lot. She was a beautiful child and a pretty girl, but she put on weight and did not take care of her physical appearance or her femininity. The fear of contracting diseases that her parents instilled in her became a fear of contracting sexually transmitted diseases. When she was physically attracted to a boy, she broke off any relationship before any physical contact. She said she was a virgin and suffered for it. Bruna tells in absolutely ego-syntonic terms that she usually shops in a big supermarket for wholesalers and buys enormous quantities of the same products. She tells me she cannot do without buying and describes a sort of trance resembling that hypnotic state described by Freud and Breuer (1893).[8] When the products she buys (food, detergent, soap, body lotions, etc.) expire (and this happens often due to the large quantities she purchases), Bruna scrupulously separates the different contents from the packaging to throw them in the appropriate containers for the separate waste collection.

Rust (2008) suggests that the increase of compulsive consumption could be a means of obscuring the ecological effects of compulsive consumption itself, leading to another vicious cycle especially because there is no strict and direct connection between consumer goods and the people who produce them, the places, the ways of exploiting production, which remain abstract and distant. For her, the main cause of our crisis (overconsumption) has become our palliative, soothing away our anxieties regarding the damage we are doing to the world.

Magnenat (2019b) posits that becoming aware of these connections means to assume a way of thinking similar to what a child has to assume for survival. The child must be able to represent the mother when she is absent and thus to make an abstraction similar to the discovery of the paternal function in the Oedipal situation.

Randall (2005, 2009) offers a clear and honest analysis of the connection between environmental anxiety, consumerism, and compulsive shopping. She praises the role of psychotherapy in dealing with defense mechanisms such as avoidance and denial by helping to recognize the losses, supporting the work of mourning at the basis of every change of attitude and giving a name to fear and anxieties.

Bruna says that she enjoys throwing away expired products. She shows a complete split between the destructiveness of the large amount of highly polluting liquids (detergents and shampoos) that she pours down the drain and how she scrupulously collects paper, metal, and glass. Although she does not seem to recognize that her consumeristic behavior, despite being rooted in a search for a saturating security, it irreparably contributes to increasing the amount of waste.[9]

One of the founders of ecopsychology, Theodore Roszak (2009), stresses that consumerism is connected to the defeat of a depression and the feeling of having a better control over one's life, when deciding what and how much to buy. It can be constituted as a way to cope with the end of a relationship or a further way of guaranteeing an experience that temporarily fills an internal void.

In the case of Bruna, I hypothesize a connection between the great amount of food her parents gave her after the death of her brother for fear of losing her and her compulsively buying enormous amounts of goods. I believe there is also a connection with her difficulty of having sexual intercourse for fear of contagion and the waste of the many products she buys. Her lack of care for herself contrasts with her attention to recycling the products she buys in excess. Only when she can get near the internal unconscious transposition of her parents' trauma over the death of their son through their too careful actions, only when she is able to recognize the anxieties of her childhood traumas and the related feeling of despair, shame, isolation, and useless rage, only then does Bruna believe she can leave the world of the dead, recognize her needs, and take care of her feminine body, a body that can become an object of affective investment. At the behavioral level, this means to lose weight, to put on make-up, and to wear better clothes. She painfully becomes aware of the guilt her parents projected onto her for something they should have prevented but did not.

Thus, Bruna begins to feel a sense of freedom from frustration, a growth in terms of autonomy, but also envy, resentment, and jealousy, all feelings she covered under a sort of omnipotent reparation. These emotions and feelings erupt in a less confused manner: until that moment, they had been frozen by the identification with her dead brother. Now they allow her an initial journey toward life, toward romantic and sexual relationships that cannot be wasted, toward a lively and vibrant world with which to get authentically and fearlessly in contact.

Notes

1 This chapter is based on my paper: Cosimo Schinaia. (2019a). Respect for the environment: Psychoanalytic reflections on the ecological crisis, *The International Journal of Psychoanalysis*, 100, 2: 272–286, copyright © 2019 Institute of Psychoanalysis. Reprinted by permission of Taylor & Francis Ltd, http://www.tandfonline.com on behalf of Institute of Psychoanalysis.

2 Melanie Klein (1946, p. 8) starts her reflections from Freudian considerations and makes them richer and more complex:

> These excrements and bad parts of the self are meant not only to injure but also to control and take possession of the object. In so far as the mother

comes to contain the bad parts of the self, she is not felt to be a separate individual to be the bad self.

3 The expression "land of fires" gets its name from the 2003 *Ecomafie* (Ecomafias) Legambiente report (see http://www.amblav.it/Download/Legambiente-Rapporto_Ecomafia2003.pdf). Roberto Saviano then used the term in his book *Gomorra* (2006). It refers to a vast area between the provinces of Naples and Caserta where organized crime (the *camorra*, in this case) illegally manages and disposes toxic waste from throughout Italy by burying it in illegal landfills and burning it, greatly damaging the agriculture, environment, and health of the residents. For these residents, there is a high risk of mortality and serious illnesses, such as breast cancer, asthma, leukemia, and congenital anomalies.

4 In comparison with the required recycling, Antonio and his family sort various types of metal and cloth.

5 In *Underworld* (1997), Don DeLillo describes for his characters something similar to the process of sorting and recycling. At home they separated their waste into glass and cans and paper products. Then they did clear glass versus colored glass. Then they did tin versus aluminum. They did plastic containers, without caps or lids, on Tuesdays only. Including garbage in separate recycling containers constitutes a specialized form of exclusion and repression in the domestic sphere.

6 *"(…) we are indignant and call it 'barbarous' (which is the opposite of civilized) when we find the paths in the Vienna Woods littered with paper"* (Freud, 1930, p. 93).

7 Revenants, or replacement children, were common in Jewish families who survived the Holocaust. They were named after the dead relative.

8 *"These (hypnotic) states share with one another and with hypnosis, however much they may differ in other respects, one common feature: the ideas which emerge in them are very intense but are cut off from associative communication with the rest of the content of consciousness"* (Freud and Breuer, 1892, p. 12).

9 Consumerism does not allow us to enjoy what we already possess; indeed, it forces us to always desire what we do not possess. Today we can reconsider one of the famous slogans of the 1970s environmental movements ("Buy, consume, die.") to show the connection between the consumption of goods and the consumption of natural resources.

Chapter 6

Wastefulness

Water can be "good" or "bad," polluted or pure, beneficial, and precious. When water cannot be consumed and there are no sewage systems, as in some areas of Africa and Asia, water can be contaminated by feces and thus by viruses, bacteria, and parasites. Water can be a mortal enemy. Washing our hands can be a simple gesture that can save our lives. The Centers for Disease Control and Prevention, the U.S. health protection agency, calls hand-cleaning the most important factor in preventing the spread of pathogens and reducing the resistance to antibiotics in health-care structures.

Transcultural anthropological studies on the role of disgust (Curtis, 2011) demonstrate how this emotion is rooted in our refusal to orally incorporate harmful objects. Valerie Curtis (2013) hypothesizes that disgust finds its origin in the avoidance of parasites. Women tend to have a lower threshold for disgust than men. This is particularly the case with pregnant women, who must protect themselves from infections and diseases more than others.

The complexity of emotional and social lives has rendered disgust wider and detached from its original preventive role. It is now an emotion-provoking refusing behaviors toward objects or substances perceived as dangerous (Miller, 1986, 1993).

In his university thesis (1841), Karl Marx argued that repulsion is the first form of self-consciousness, as the function of disgust is to preserve the self.

Throughout his work, Freud notes that disgust is a reaction-formation not only toward genital desires but also toward some infantile sexual impulses as coprophilia, demonstrating that sexual libido investments can convert to disgust because sex is felt as dirty and polluting.

It is fundamental for our health and survival to protect ourselves from pathogens. According to Foucault (1984), in Ancient Greece, a reasonable existence could not unfold without a frame for the "health practice" (ευγενία πραγμάτεια or τέχνη) that was a permanent fixture of daily life. This frame allowed knowing at every moment what was to be done and how to do it. This practice needed a medical perception of the world, or at least of the space and circumstances in which a person lived. In the same book, Foucault also describes obsessive introversion and excessive attention to the

DOI: 10.4324/9781003220077-7

idea of purifying hygiene, an idea that seduced the elites of the post-classical age and became an ideal and pervasive norm of life.

However, today we see the triumph of hyper-hygiene, a sort of rupophobia. In a consumerist and fetishist way, this prescribes appearance, aesthetics, and narcissism. Advertising for cosmetics and personal- and home-hygiene products focuses on how aesthetic appearance can positively influence our social relationships. Parallel to appearance and the search for immediately recognizable social status, advertising promotes the excessive intake of water. Italy leads most countries in water consumption: every Italian citizen consumes about 245 liters of drinking water per day, according to the Italian National Institute of Statistics.

We are so convinced of the falsehood that drinking water, a beneficial and necessary good, is limitless and so we use it too much. We are so influenced by media-driven campaigns for absolute cleanliness that we risk becoming rupophobic,[1] afraid to get anything soiled, to show dirt, to reveal those bad things inside of us, but also to be contaminated from contact with others, with people who are different from us.

Water is a precious and exhaustible good that must be protected wisely so that it can be sufficient for the entire world population, in particular, in those dry seasons that frequently occur in the Mediterranean because of the lack of rain.

We do not turn taps on and off according to our actual necessities. What represents the Western lifestyle if not brushing our teeth, flushing the toilet,[2] showering every time we want, running half-empty washing machines and dishwashers just to clean a few things? Everything tends to the waste of a good that is scarce not only in other areas of the world but also in some Western countries, at least in some seasons.

When I was a young physician specializing in psychiatry, I worked at a school as a doctor. I discovered that parents were so scared to find lice eggs in their children's hair that they made them shower and shampoo daily, in a sort of ritual. The effect was a Munchausen syndrome by proxy,[3] a rupophobia acquired through a mechanism of identification. The harshness of hair products and excessive cleaning, as suggested by an old television advertisement, caused dehydration, itching, and erythema, sometimes reactive seborrhea.

The problem is not progress. Progress brought us drainage systems, watertight pipeline aqueducts, pasteurization, vaccines, disinfectants, and detergents, a drastic reduction in infectious disease. But the other side of progress is its consumerist perversion.

For Stefano Mistura (2001), appearance prevails over reality because the relationship with the substituted object, that is, the fetish, precedes and does not allow any relationship with real beings. We are surrounded by fetishes, objects to which we attribute qualities that they do not possess *per se*, and that, because of these qualities, they look different from what really are.

Inert objects take on life form and, thanks to their fascinating power, prevail over people, who gradually lose the vitality of their bodies and become so rigid as to become mere things. The modern shopping mall is a paradigmatic example of the great power of objects: the merest of glances at the universality of goods progressively annihilates the individual will and atrophies a person's capacity to reflect.

In Frédéric Beigbeder's novel £ 9.99, the main character (who is into advertising similar to the author) says that, in his profession, no one wishes people happiness because happy people do not consume.

Freud (1930, p. 93) writes:

> Dirtiness of any kind seems to us incompatible with civilization. We extend our demand for cleanliness to the human body too. (...) Indeed, we are not surprised by the idea of setting up the use of soap as an actual yardstick of civilization.

On the one hand, it is right to protect ourselves from infection and disease and to avoid escaping into an anti-modernist catastrophism that denies the past and the myriad scientific and technological discoveries that have ameliorated the human condition throughout time. On the other, it is paramount to enjoy progress but to avoid exceeding, wasting, and refusing those cultural attitudes that promote appearance and superficiality, casting aside substance and authenticity.

Excessive consumption and water waste are also determined by many other factors, such as industry, agriculture, factory farming, urban sewage systems, and it is crucial to intervene. Just the same, a radical change in our habits and lifestyle would help to restore ecological balance.

Jun'ichirō Tanizaki (1933) writes that we must not fear dirt if only because it is not unusual that what is beautiful in certain objects partially depends on their greasiness or sordidness.

Lynch (1990) offers a different perspective. Animals spend copious amounts of time sorting and cleaning their nests. Among social animals, this basic behavior involves peace, courtship, or social links. Similarly, a good number of human beings spend their time cleaning – washing their bodies, food, and clothes; tidying their homes – that is, cleansing themselves and their surroundings. Some of these activities have become social symbols, sometimes even religious rituals of purification. Eliminating waste can be seen as a degrading action, especially if it constitutes a person's primary activity. Nonetheless, the act of cleaning (separating good from waste) can be respectable, even pleasurable. An example here is showering.

Of course, I do not want to extol the virtues of filth. But I think it is necessary to reconsider our concept of hygiene, a concept that, when exaggerated, can be seen as the modest stepson of morality (Salomé, 1958). We must assess the neurotic and defensive features of hygiene to safeguard its enjoyable and healthy features. Fighting the dirt of home and body has always been a daily task even when we lived in caves. This is an aspect we share with the other animals, which clear away leftovers and excreta from their burrows and nests. Felines lick to wash themselves. Elephants use their proboscises to shower. Birds devote considerable amounts of time to wetting and smoothing their feathers. Chimpanzees clean one another's fur, a behavior known as grooming: it is calculated that they spent a fifth of their lives this way.

The anthropologist Virginia Smith (2018) reminds us that from prehistoric times, human beings have been removing waste and malodorous material, controlling both their aspect and their smell, demonstrating an instinctive need to feel clean.

All this said, we must contrast those consumerist aberrations that, according to an ideological and commercial perspective, pervert and misunderstand the original concept of hygiene.

Clinical vignette – *Noli me tangere* (do not touch me)

When she comes to a session, Delia is always irreproachable. Before leaving home, she takes a shower, changes clothes, and applies copious amounts of perfume. She does not intend to meet me dirty and untidy. When she hangs her coat on the hook, Delia takes care to put it over already hooked clothes, and before entering the consulting room, she goes to the bathroom to wash her hands.[4] Once in the consulting room, she shakes my hand almost in passing, a hand chapped and ruined from overwashing, as if she wishes to avoid any ritual that implies bodily contact. When she lays down, she expertly avoids putting her shoes on the carpet at the end of the couch by awkwardly slipping down so she can dangle off her feet of it.

Delia comes from a family she defines as "alternative" and "hippie." Her parents used to wander around the house naked and leave doors open, even the bathroom door. For them, privacy had no value in the name of a libertarian and community ideal that Delia had been unable to accept. She felt confused, but also angry for what she defines a cosmic disorder, for she could not have a place all on her own even in the most intimate moments.

Before meeting me, Delia had some sessions with a psychotherapist who asked her to lay down on a living room couch. She ended that therapy after a while because she often fantasized about her therapist having coffee with guests on that couch. That is, she did not think it possible for that couch to provide that non-provisional, private, and an all-to-herself place that she desired. She wanted a place with a precise function. Furthermore, she felt disgusted thinking she had to put her head where strangers had put their rear ends.

From the beginning of university, her hands began to profusely sweat and she felt nausea when in public or unknown places. Thus, she started to avoid other people's homes, cafés, movie theaters, and classrooms.

> Sometimes, however, concurrent circumstances bring about an abnormal somatic phenomenon in which the excitation is discharged. Thus there may be vomiting where the feeling of uncleanness produces a physical feeling of nausea (…).
>
> (Freud and Breuer, 1892–1895, p. 210)

She is greatly distressed by the simple idea of people seeing her sweating hands when she is out of the house – when saying hello by shaking hands, as is common in social relationships – or her face when she tries to control the impulse to vomit. She also feels ashamed, which makes every potentially enjoyable social activity a sort of agony. When she goes out, she asks her father to drive her and always controls the distance she has to travel to avoid meetings she perceives as dangerous, in case she has to shake hands to introduce herself or greet someone. Her fear of hyperhidrosis and emesis dissipates once she is at home, which she defines as her "shell," and has no reason to go out.

She suffers greatly for the impossibility of simple physical contact with others. Throughout the years, none of the many medical examinations she underwent revealed an organic or bodily pathology. Nonetheless, the physicians' responses do not satisfy Delia, who is pinning her hopes on a physical disease to explain her plight. On the one hand, she is suspicious of a psychological cause for her difficulties; on the other, she seeks my help because she does not have many alternatives and would not permit her problems to ruin a significant romantic relationship.

Delia fears that her relationship will not last because of her sweaty hands and her worries about vomiting. She is scared of both the possibility of contact and the impossibility of contact. She says that her boyfriend is tender and respectful but, at the same time, she defines him as superficial and dismissive. In fact, he tends to minimize each discomfort she feels or every reflection she proposes, he appears unable to give them any emotional character.

He does not seem capable of fully understanding her difficulties. He minimizes and underestimates not only her difficulties but also his. It was the same for her father who, when he had to face a difficult situation, always said it was nothing. For her boyfriend, her sweating hands were not a problem: he takes, tightens, kindly caresses them. But he does not reassure her: he does not understand that she suffers, feels dirty, and she must go find a place to wash her hands and eliminate the fat from her skin.

Delia fears each approach is insistent and intrusive and is afraid of getting dirty from contact with others, who provoke her impulse to vomit, and from the greasiness of her internal world. She washes her hands many times a day

and takes many showers with perfumed soap. This ritual is highly sophisticated: after the shower, Delia takes a bath. This is because with the shower
she avoids seeing the dirt that could float in the bathtub. Showers consume
less water than baths. This is not a problem for Delia: shower plus bath, she
must purify herself, not see and smell the dirt, contrarily to Roi Soleil, about
whom *"we are astonished to learn of the objectionable smell which emanated
(...)"* (Freud 1930, p. 93).

Similar to Ferenczi (1928), who defined the sense of touch as the capacity
for empathy, Glauco Carloni (1984) highlights how, in addition to feeling
and experiencing through the tactile, we observe, feel, and study how the
other is disposed, structured, and influenced by his vulnerability. The psychic makes use of the physical as well as of the other four senses and that
sixth sense we call "empathy."

Delia slowly passes from difficulty at being approached, even delicately,
to showing her need for dependence, something that could expose her to
sadistic intrusions, to the possibility of trusting me, to feeling that she has
a place of her own in the consulting room, that she can be touched empath-
ically, but without any sort of excitement, touched through words that at
the same time move her and move me. The words are like music, they act on
her feelings and provoke bodily sensations. By using an embodied language
in the analytic relationship (Quinodoz, 2002), Delia can be accepted as she
actually is, without resorting to more sophisticated and less valued contacts.

Luce Irigaray (2011) promotes a new way of knowing, able to consider
the relevance of touch in the constitution of our personal individuation and
relationships with others.

Delia slowly passes from the difficulty of feeling approached, even if very
carefully, a position that does not permit her to express her need for that
dependence that would expose her to sadistic intrusions, to the feeling of
being able to trust, to the reassurance that the consulting room can be her
place. In this place, she can be touched with empathy but without excitement, through words that move and resonate, words that, similar to music,
act on feelings and cause bodily sensations.

Delia feels that our meetings allow for the acceptance of her sweating
hands and impulse to vomit and recognize them as cognitive and emotional
representations of her difficulties: they cannot be denied or paternalistically
underestimated as a trifling or irrelevant problem. This allows Delia to begin to recount the repeated sexual abuse her uncle perpetrated on her when
she was a teenager.

Her uncle was highly respected in the family, especially by her father,
who considered him the paragon of ethical virtue. During her adolescence,
the uncle would enter Delia's room and force her to caress his penis until he
ejaculated on her face. Then he would lick the sperm from her face and vo-
luptuously kiss her. Delia reports with embarrassment that in that moment
she would smile: to resist disgust and fear, she used fantasy to represent that
ejaculating penis as a splitting clumsy puppet.

Speaking for the first time of her trauma without her father's minimizations (which she experiences as irresponsible and unable to protect her from the seductive trauma) permits us to slowly connect her impulses to vomit to these painful events and to the anxiety of getting soiled and licked (like a bitch, she says). We connect the sweating of her hands to the fear that her internal world (which she experienced as filthy and ignoble) can emerge and infect others, but also that others can soil and infect her, as occurred during the sexual abuse.

In *Inhibition, Symptoms and Anxiety* (1926, p. 88) Freud writes:

> (...) the defensive symptom of disgust (...), arising originally as a deferred reaction to the experiencing of a passive sexual act, appears later whenever the idea of such an act is presented.

Delia reports that she is very happy to have reduced the number of showers, baths, and hand washings, and to be able to shake my hand when she arrives and leaves the consulting room. She says she remains a bit suspicious about doing this, but no longer feels ashamed and disgusted.

Delia's case demonstrates how individual lifestyle, here characterized by excessive water use, can depend on affective, phantasmatic, and painful personal experiences, and the revival of unsolved emotional conflict. Allowing close but protected contact with deep trauma, thanks to their working through permits not only a calmer existence but also better environmental attitudes and behaviors. It is not about magically making anxieties disappear, but rather about creating a relational situation to render anxieties recognizable and acceptable, by respecting individual rhythms, and favoring the development of constructive thinking.

Wasting heat

Today, we know ample about what causes outdoor air pollution, for example, from vehicles, industry, and home heating systems[5] that constantly emit gases, mainly CO_2, and damage the ecosystem, especially in urban areas. We know less about the so-called indoor pollution, the air contamination in indoor environments generated by chemical, physical, and biological pollutants.

Indoor or domestic air pollution triggers diseases with various degrees of severity, such as asthma, lung disease, allergies, and legionellosis (Goldmann, 2019).

The scientific journalist Emily Anthes (2020) points out that modern humans, in particular, North Americans and Europeans, are an indoor species, as they spend 90% of their time indoors,[6] at homes, workplaces, schools, shops, restaurants, gyms, hospitals, and prisons. In these spaces, air quality and adequate ventilation are crucial factors. Aeration and ventilation replace the air in a house with fresh air from the outside. A few minutes are sufficient for this operation.

The main sources of indoor pollution are tobacco smoke, gas stoves, wood-burning ovens, fireplaces, heating systems in general and kerosene in particular, cleaning products (solvents and detergents), building material and insulation, as well as emissions of harmful substances from electronic instruments such as printers.

We can decide whether the air circulating inside the home can be purified according to environmental, domestic, and individual sustainability. Plants can help, for example, dracaena, epipremnum, gerbera, ficus, and aloe. Beyond their ornamental function, they naturally absorb and reduce indoor or domestic pollution by filtering air and eliminating poisons in it.

If the air is stale, the environment is unhealthy, our reflexes slow down and our behaviors change due to the lack of oxygen. Known as Sick Building Syndrome, this can be found in new or recently renovated buildings. The most common symptoms are ear, nose, and throat irritation, hypersensitivity, allergies, tiredness, and headaches. The feeling of comfort thermo-hygrometric depends on body temperature and the degree of humidity of the skin that must always be low. The amygdala should signal us the excess of heat as a dangerous element for our survival. Unfortunately, cultural features related to the pleasure of a prolonged summer – the aesthetics of tanned bodies and the ease of finding heat in a closed environment as social status (things promoted by seductive advertising) – prevail, confound, and modify our basal physiological responses to external stimuli. For example, if we feel cold, we tend to increase the temperature of our environment instead of covering up. Our attention, vigilance, reaction time, mental calculation, and motivation decrease when the temperature is too high (over 32°C), whereas aggression, feelings of alarm, and physical disturbances related to the thermal shock between inside and outside increase (Goldmann, Redaelli and Cerveglieri, 2019).

There is a connection between the quality of internal spaces of a building, their design and luminosity, and the presence of great windows opening to green areas and psychophysical well-being and thus the happiness of their inhabitants (Anthes, 2020).

Clinical vignette – no more woolen vest!

Oreste is an only child. He was born when his parents were quite old, after many years of infertility treatments. After multiple unsuccessful treatments, his parents accepted the idea of being childless, so the birth of Oreste had been unexpected, not completely accepted, basically unscheduled. They felt guilt for having lost the desire to become parents and so they went overboard: they were hyper-protective, excessively attentive, always fearful that he would fall ill. Oreste says that they are two very good nurses than two loving parents.

Since he can remember, he has always worn a woolen vest throughout the year. In winter, he wears a vest with long sleeves, and in summer, the one with short sleeves. His parents granted him all his wishes, except for playing football with other kids, going to the swimming pool and, more in general, participating in sports and sweating. His father taught him the quiet game of chess, a game he is very good at. He excelled at school, but he felt marginalized by his peers, who did not make fun of him but judged him as too calm and noticed that he was not available for outdoor games and sports. He lived with his family in a small town in the Ligurian Riviera until he went to medical school. His parents rented an elegant, centrally located, and comfort-filled apartment for him in the city where he attended school.

When he began to live alone, Oreste openly rebelled against his parents for the first time in his life: he threw away all the heavy clothes he was forced to wear. Of course, the first to be tossed out was the woolen vest, but he did the same to all the clothes he felt were oppressing. He began to be completely naked in the apartment, with the temperature raised and the windows constantly closed. This act of rebellion against his parents' hyper-protection slowly transformed into a lifestyle that was incompatible with social relationships and environmental stewardship.[7] In class, he began the slow ritual of undressing. First, he took off his coat, then, his jacket, next, his sweater, and another sweater, finally, his shirt, and remained with a T-shirt. He complained about the temperature in the classroom being low, but he felt it impossible to put some of his clothes back on.

When he starts his analysis, Oreste suffers chronic bronchitis and has no significant social relationships.

Once in the consulting room, he repeats the same ritual described above. In his T-shirt, he asks me if, since I am a physician, he can also take off his pants and stay in his underwear only. A bit perplexed and confused, I ask if he feels too hot, but he says no. He even points out that it is necessary to increase the room temperature because he feels cold. I interpret this as him displacing his intense need for warmth, he is unable to find in the human beings with a temperature increase by metal heaters. That is, he is unable to give value to his autonomy in thermoregulation and his capacity to protect himself from the cold, he prefers to give this value not to the relationship with other human beings, something very painful for him, but to that with metal heaters.

His parents' apprehensive but affectively cold behavior taught him that warmth could be obtained by avoiding contact: his parents manifested warmth through a woolen vest and generous gifts. Unlike authentic human warmth, he could manage his parents' apprehension as he desired, similarly to what can be done with a thermostat or a heater control knob. Temperature management permitted him to express his childhood, triumphant, and narcissistic omnipotence. He could not change and adapt to true environmental conditions – the presence of others, a fundamental dimension for determining the temperature of relationships – without resorting to devices.

Nonetheless, recognizing the limit imposed by the presence of others would have meant the end of his narcissistic part, which would have been substituted by a conscious acceptance of reality. He was born from a distant desire that waned over time: how many times did his parents tell him that he was unexpected, the "son of chance!" They felt a strong and rigid sense of responsibility toward him for having brought him into the world. This transformed into a form of anxious but affectively sterile worry, a reaction to their sense of guilt. It is necessary to be beloved, desired, and understood to observe and comprehend ourselves and the surrounding world. Unfortunately, since he was a child, he felt resentment toward his parents: he experienced them as oppressive and unable to recognize and satisfy his desire for human warmth. He unconsciously and consciously reacted by exhibiting a collusive submission that became resistance and then transgression against authority.

Oreste brings into the consulting room the same emotional situation he experienced early in the relationship with his parents and later represented in his apartment and the medical school classroom.

Once I forgot to air out the consulting room before his session. Oreste could smell the cheap perfume of the preceding patient. He was sure she was a prostitute. To keep his apartment warm, he always kept the windows closed, so that there was always a bad smell. He recognized this but justified it by arguing that it was his authentic and personal smell, incomparable to other smells. He defined it "the smell of a barn:" a non-neutral and non-aseptic condition, a warm and safe place, as in the Christian nativity barn.

Oreste reports many fantasies about being a fetus again, returning to a place where every one of us once dwelled, the warm maternal uterus.

Freud (1900, p. 399) writes:

> In some dreams of landscapes or other localities emphasis is laid in the dream itself on a convinced feeling of having been there once before. (Occurrences of 'déjà vu' in dreams have a special meaning.) These places are invariably the genitals of the dreamer's mother; there is indeed no other place about which one can assert with such conviction that one has been there once before.

Freud (1930, p. 91) returns to this topic:

> (...) and the dwelling-house was a substitute for the mother's womb, the first lodging, for which in all likelihood man still longs, and in which he was safe and felt at ease.

In the analysis of the Wolfman (1918) Freud observes that the interiors of the intrauterine existence appear as warm containers but, at the same time, are at the basis of the uncanny, that is, they are both a refuge of inevitably and incestuously unrealized desires and a potential crypt for burying human beings. He (1919, p. 245) writes that the mother's sex organ or body can be experienced and interpreted as uncanny, even if they were familiar at the beginning: *"In this case too, then, the 'unheimlich' is what was once heimlich, familiar (...)."*

Oreste transformed his apartment from a protective shelter from the storm to a microenvironment under his total control, a hermetically sealed box, a container precluding every exchange between inside and outside, a sort of crypt in which it became increasingly impossible to live or breathe.

The slow and difficult construction of an outspoken but comfortable analytic relationship allows Oreste to learn new and unknown sensory abilities and direct relationships with the environmental dynamics, to dress more adequately, at least according to the season, to withstand the presence of smells different from his, to stop abusing his home heating system and to open his apartment windows. The smell of his closed apartment, which he initially experienced as protective, is now so disturbing, annoying, and *unheimlich* that he opens the windows and is able to better manage the home heating system.

In both cases, it had been necessary to make a twofold intervention: recognize the influence of the past over the present and, once the oppressive childhood anxieties had been worked through, recognize the harm, in environmental terms, of his behavior and try to modify it.

Notes

1 "Rupophobia" and "misophobia" define the fear of coming into contact with dirt and thus getting contaminated by germs. This fear leads the person to assume exaggerated and obsessive preventative measures in personal and home hygiene. "Aphephobia" defines the disgust of coming into contact with certain objects such as hair.

2 In 2006, Ken Livingstone, then mayor of London, invited his constituents to not flush the toilet every time they urinated.

3 Munchausen syndrome by proxy is a mental disorder whereby parents (generally mothers) attract attention by making up or causing illness in their children. The DSM-V (2013) includes it in the category of "fictitious disorders" as "factitious disorder imposed on another."

4 Breuer and Freud (1893–1895, p. 245n) write:

> Some observations lead us to believe that the fear of touching, or, more properly, the fear of being dirtied, which compels women to keep on washing their hands all the time, very often has this derivation. Their washing is derived from the same mental process as Lady Macbeth's" [Macbeth, "Go get some water/And wash this filthy witness from your hand.
>
> (2.2.60–61)]

5 In *Un pianeta ad aria condizionata* (An air-conditioned planet) (2019), Antonio Cianciullo points out how global warming makes us protect ourselves in small air-conditioned forts such as homes, cars, and offices. This generates a significant increase in electricity consumption and releases heat in the public environment.

6 During the COVID-19 isolation, it reached almost 100%.

7 In urban areas, home heating systems contribute six times more CO_2 emissions than traffic does.

Chapter 7

Light and noise pollution

Light pollution is an alteration of the light levels naturally present at night. It causes various kinds of environmental, scientific, cultural, and economic damages.

Environmental damage includes difficulty or loss of orientation in some animals (migratory birds, sea turtles, and nocturnal moths); alteration of circadian rhythms with consequent mood disturbances in humans as well as plants, which can anticipate blossoming, and animals (some birds sing before dusk, the predator–prey relationship is modified). The economic damage concerns the costs of energy waste; the scientific one relates to difficulties caused by astronomical research. The principal cultural damage is due to the disappearance of the starry sky in the most polluted countries.[1]

In his *Zibaldone* (September 20, 1821), Giacomo Leopardi writes about the pleasure of viewing light in cities. Here, light is dappled by shadows and contrasts with the dark; light fades gradually, as on roofs, secluded places, hiding the shining star from view. The pleasure is in its variety, uncertainty, in the fact that you cannot see everything and therefore you are able to wander using imagination through things unseen.

Francesca Rigotti (2020) denounces the disappearance of the dark due to light pollution and proposes an imaginary and metaphorical path that can re-evaluate the "knowledge of the dark." This knowledge includes, for example, the great topic of the blindness as a form of foresight (vision prophecy) that the ancients believed that in some way it compensated for (and even surpassed) the material loss of sight. Examples in this sense are characters, including Oedipus or the blind fortune teller, Tiresias.

Pope Francis (2015) says that we make every effort to adapt to our environment, but when it is disorderly, chaotic, or saturated with noise and ugliness, such overstimulation makes it difficult to find ourselves integrated and happy.

DOI: 10.4324/9781003220077-8

In his *Science of Logic*, Friedrich Hegel (1812–1816) writes that one can see just as little in pure light as in pure darkness. Pure light and pure darkness are two voids, which are the same thing.

The interdependence, interconnection, and complementarity of light and darkness are underrated topics in Western thought and culture, at least since the Age of Enlightenment.

Although the Indian writer Amitav Ghosh[2] (2016) stresses that modernity is not a "virus" spread from Western civilization to the rest of the world, undoubtedly some perceptions, such as that of darkness, have had different destinies and representations in different parts of the world.

In Praise of Shadows (1933) by the Japanese writer Jun'ichirō Tanizaki focuses on the appeal of the shadow, endangered by the spread of the Western way of life. This way of living is characterized by an excess of electric illumination. Tanizaki goes against the dominion of light, often violent and indiscreet, and lauds the aesthetic of semi-darkness that guarantees intimacy, quiet, and relaxation. He praises the beauty of old farms, tearooms, solitary mountain temples, traditional toilettes far from the house and immersed in shadow, in great contrast with the modern need for brightness and hygiene; silverware, which, unlike in the West where it is continuously polished so it glitters, in Japan acquires aesthetic value when the patina of time makes it dark.

Not in the thing itself but in the degree of shadow lies beauty for Tanizaki. He highlights how our Western civilization, daily life, and idea of pleasure are based on the hyper-development of some senses to the detriment of others, never an attempt to harmonize our senses.

How Western civilization opposes darkness! This is evident in Dante Alighieri's *Divine Comedy* (*Inferno*, 1, 1–3, 1314) that starts with a description of a gloomy wood in the midway of our mortal life.

The gloomy wood is at the gates of hell. It can be found also in Virgil's *Aeneid* (VI, 179), an inspiration for Dante, and represents chaos and disorder (Edwards, 2018).

Darkness is represented negatively in Francisco Goya's black paintings (*pinturas negras*)[3] and in Joseph Conrad's novel *Heart of Darkness* (1899).[4]

Conrad defines dark as not only the hostile world of the tropical river forest but also the evil that dwells in the human soul. He argues that the most bitter illusion and the murkiest darkness of a society is to believe it is bringing civilization to the heart of Africa but, in reality, it only brings colonialism and destruction.[5]

Paolo Mauri (2007) posits that the word "light" has positive features, whereas "dark" or "obscure" refer to its opposite. He points out that evil seems obscure when we do not know its real causes. Night is the place of evil in an infinite series of legends in the most diverse traditions. At night, sinister spirits and vampires circulate and are forced to hide at dawn with the return of the light.

But the positive meaning and value of darkness can be found in the writing at the entrance of the Sacro Speco monastery in Subiaco, near Montecassino Abbey[6]:

Lumina si quaeris, Benedicte, quid eligis antra?
Quaesiti servant luminis antra nihil.
Sed perge in tenebris radiorum quaerere lucem,
nonnisi ab oscura sidera nocte micant.[7]

Having intuited the value of darkness, Benedict anticipated the fight against light pollution, to which all cities have fallen victim, so much so that, according to a 2007 UNESCO resolution, contemplating the firmament should be considered an inalienable right of humankind. Movements in favor of the dark sky are increasing all over the world: Italy, for example, has dedicated a day for promoting for saving energy, called *"Mi illumino di meno"* (I illuminate myself less), inspired by the verses of Giuseppe Ungaretti's "Mattina," *"M'illumino/d'immenso"* (I illuminate myself/with immensity). The day takes place every February 16, the day the Kyoto Protocol went into effect.

The Finnish architect Juhani Pallasmaa (2004) invokes the need to go against the growing hegemony of sight, that oculcentrism, that purevisibilism Le Corbusier promoted, according to which vision assumes a central role in Western civilization.[8] He argues that this hegemony is responsible for an alienating, abstracting, and distancing architecture, not one that promotes the positive sensations coming from entrenchment, intimacy, and affinity.

Even the architect Henry Plummer (2016) moves away from the negative visions of Goya and Conrad and toward the vision of Benedict of Nursia, when he praises the surprising possibility of darkness to transform a static reality into a less defined one, to make light glow more magnetically, to render elusive spaces more adventurous. Darkness affords us supplementary potential to discover unknown and unseen elements.

Great psychoanalysts such as Freud, Bion, and Lacan praised the value of darkness.

Freud uses the metaphor of darkness in his May 25, 1916 letter to Lou Andreas-Salomé (Freud, 1916a, p. 45):

I know that in writing I have to blind myself artificially in order to focus all the light on one dark spot, renouncing cohesion, harmony, rhetoric, and everything which you call symbolic; (...) my eyes, adapted as they are to the dark, probably can't stand strong light or an extensive range of vision.

Bion (1990, p. 20) reconsiders Freud's words:

> Instead of trying to bring a brilliant, intelligent, knowledgeable light to bear on obscure problems, I suggest we bring to bear a diminution of the 'light' – a penetrating beam of darkness: a reciprocal of the searchlight. The peculiarity of this penetrating ray is that it could be directed towards the object of our curiosity, and this object would absorb whatever light already existed, leaving the area of examination exhausted of any light that it possessed. The darkness would be so absolute that it would achieve a luminous, absolute vacuum. So that, if any object existed, however, faint, it would show up very clearly.

In turn, Lacan (1964, p. 102) writes:

> If you wish to see a star of the fifth or sixth size, do not look straight at it – this is known as the Arago phenomenon. You will be able to see it only if you fix your eye to one side.

Calvino (1988) makes us notice that when there is too much to see, we cannot see anything and we end up losing the power of bringing visions into focus with our eyes shut and thus thinking in terms of images.

Clinical vignette – and soon the darkness

Michele is a patient of mine who shows obsessive and controlling aspects in the initial moments of our first meeting. When he enters the consulting room, he visually verifies that everything in the room is in place. He checks that the light is turned on so that he can notice with a quick but attentive look that every object in the room is stably distributed. At home, the lights are always turned on night and day: he says that it is to keep away criminals and to make it easier for him to move about at night.

When he brings dreams to our sessions, Michele feels obliged to describe and explain them in detail. He defines them as illuminating and he likes to interpret them. He usually devalues and minimizes my comments with the expression, "Yes, but...," which reduces the explanatory and emotional power of my own comments and serves as a launch point for further do-it-yourself interpretation. During an evening session, while recounting a dream, he defines as illuminating because it offers new (and for him unthinkable until that moment) ways to comprehend his relational difficulties, the light goes out, leaving us surrounded in sudden total darkness, making Michele's and my context strange. We cannot take anything for granted.

According to Mauri (2007), we fear blackouts precisely because we cannot control the total dark, a dark that is worse than that of the old and controllable natural night.

My first impulse would have been to check the electric meter. But Michele's unexpected reaction has me glued to my chair. I choose not to intervene. I do not interpret the situation with a preconceived meaning. I choose to directly face the change in the physical and relational field. I bet on Michele's and my capacity to deal with a novelty occurring outside our will. I could expect the emergence of anxiety in Michele because of the lack of visual control. But Michele is not upset by the dark. In a calm and satisfied voice, he tells me: "Finally we are equal. I don't see you when I come here, now you cannot see me. Our meeting is now on the equal ground. We are both blind and scared."

I do not feel these words as indicating a competition, but rather a demand for a deeper understanding of his anxiety. He wants me to be able to comprehend his discomfort in the same way as he feels it. Darkness allows me to do so symmetrically, equally.

In *Inhibitions, Symptoms, and Anxiety* (1926, p. 124) Freud writes:

> If we cannot see things clearly, we will at least see clearly what the obscurities are.

Michele tells me his illuminating dream. He entered a tunnel with a flashlight and, when he lost all hope to reach the end of the tunnel because the flashlight was becoming increasingly dim, he heard the meowing of a kitten that slowly but decidedly approached him and started rubbing against him, curling up, and purring. When the torch stopped working, Michele saw that the kitten's eyes were shining. He feels touched by this scene and cries when he describes it.

The dream ended with a feeble and distant light appearing at the end of the tunnel. The light allows Michele to orientate and save himself and the kitten. Unlike all previous sessions, Michele does not comment on the dream in a pedantic manner. He remains silent.

In this moment, in the dark room, we feel a sort of perplexity and insecurity because we have lost the usual spatial and temporal coordinates. I, too, feel heartened by the emotionally intense childish aspects Michele brought with his dream.

Inside of me, Michele is now the young man who wanted to make me feel his anxieties and the scared and vulnerable child represented by the meowing kitten.

The disappearance of light favors the emergence of an anxiety that could be shared. Michele was able to put this anxiety inside of me and to set his intellectualized and opinionated aspects outside the consulting room. These aspects were typical of his sessions and led him to define his dreams as illuminating, in the sense that he would have been able to illuminate me with his explanations and clarifications. Now he can finally show the unexpected ability to communicate and to remain in silent contact with his childhood emotions that we are able to discuss even after the return of the light. Only in the dark could Michele directly experience a non-competitive meeting with the analyst.

Federico Flegenheimer borrows a metaphor from Maurice Merleau-Ponty and compares the psychoanalytic setting to the dark in a cinema (Nissim Momigliano, 1988).[9] In this case, we take the dark for granted, a sort of darkroom of the unconscious, but it is a necessary condition for enjoying a movie.

As in José Saramago's novel *Blindness* (1995), the coming of the dark somehow allows us to measure the world and society, so the dark in my consulting room suddenly modified the setting and allowed Michele to report his dream without any competitive intellectualization. He felt that we were equal, blind, and perhaps more sensitive to analytic work. The dark surrounded us and permitted us to increase our senses. It freed me of the need to understand everything and to interpret the various features of Michele's dream. I could allow "(...) the process (...) of awareness of incoherent elements and the individual's ability to tolerate that awareness" (Bion, 1992, p. 195), in short, to blind myself to enjoy with him the encounter of his childish parts without the mediation of artificial light. We were both enlightened by the kitten's glittering eyes.

In referring to John Keats' letter of December 21, 1817, to his brothers, Bion (1992, p. 125) speaks of *"(...) Negative Capability, that is, when a man is capable of being in uncertainties, mysteries, doubts, without any irritable reaching after fact and reason."*

James S. Grotstein (2007, p. 1) remembers this event:

> Once, following an analytic session of mine, Bion, out of character, went to the bookshelf, pulled out a German edition of Freud's correspondence with Lou Andreas-Salomé, and translated it for me on the spot. I made notes about it moments afterwards: 'When conducting an analysis, one must cast a beam of intense darkness[10] so that something which has hitherto been obscured by the glare of the illumination can glitter all the more in the darkness.'

Sometimes the attention to relevant phenomena lights the blinding lamp of Psyche that not only blinds us but also burns our skin. Once lit, the lamp of Psyche does not allow us to see aspects that we do not yet know or do not want to know because they scare us and bring disturbing elements into the consulting room (Ferruta, 2008).

Mauri (2007) enters the metaphor of light to leave the Platonic sun at the top of all ideas and return into the cave where the slave exited and returned to tell his friends that he left what is light and what is darkness, what it means to pass from darkness to light, and what light-induced blindness is. Darkness is associated with what it is not yet revealed, perhaps what can never be revealed. If darkness is infinity, light defines, softens, and builds paths and trajectories.

The appearance of darkness in the consulting room permitted authentic contact with something disturbing. Darkness fostered the transformation of the disturbing into something domestic and familiar. It created the conditions for establishing trust and collaboration in the analyst–analysand couple at work.

Noise pollution

Noise pollution is caused by excessive exposure to high-intensity sound and noise. This can occur in cities and nature. Italian law n. 447/1995, art. 2 provides this definition of noise pollution:

> The introduction of noise into residential or external environments such as to cause annoyance or disturbance to repose and human activities, danger to human health, deterioration of ecosystems, material goods, and monuments, or to interfere with the normal function of these environments.

The most notable causes of noise pollution include:

– Domestic activity. This generates a large and unexpected amount of noise. Inappropriate use of appliances (televisions, washing machines, dishwashers, air conditioners, etc.) significantly determines the amount of noise that a house produces
– Car, rail, and air traffic
– Industrial and construction sites
– Shared spaces. Sounds or music in shared or public spaces, such as bars, restaurants, airports, malls, swimming pools, and beaches, can disturb, bother, and annoy, depending on specific individual sensitivity. Even passive exposure to low-volume music, which could not be classified as annoying per se, can be subjectively perceived as such. An example is the forced and involuntary listening to background music.

Our lives are perpetually immersed in a permanent soundtrack, Nicoletta Polla-Mattiot (2017) points out, with our every daily activity accompanied by a specific sound. It is not only traffic and the noise of the metropolis, but a kind of ubiquitous piped-in music that emits trills, buzzes, and musical sounds, with loudspeakers and sound-emitting gadgets always on, telephones, beeps, and entertainment that follows us everywhere, in the supermarket, the underground parking, the waiting room, the plane – everywhere and every time.

By intruding into privacy and intimacy over time, noise pollution can cause hearing loss, sleep disorders, psychophysical discomfort, and stress caused by high levels of cortisol in the blood.

Carlo Emilio Gadda (1959), not only a writer but also an engineer, lists with bitter irony, alongside indubitable advantages, the countless disadvantages of the noise pollution of modern building techniques. The home protects and defends us against the stresses and strains of modern life. We need rest and sleep, as well as food and air; we use our neuro-encephalic system, brain, and spinal cord every minute of our lives in the struggle of daily living. Today's home is unable to preserve and defend us and our nervous system from these stresses and strains. The cement structure made of bricks, resounds like a drum, forcing us to hear every noise, every note, and syllable of the structure.

Our senses perceive a plethora of stimuli that emanate from the environment and influence our mind at different levels. If these stimuli are of poor quality, their variety does not compensate for their harmfulness.

A project of the University of Naples called "Clips. Corpora e lessici di italiano parlato e scritto" (Clips. Bodies and lexicons of spoken and written Italian)[11] assesses how the Italian language changed in the past 50 years. It evolved more at the lexical than the rhythmical level, that is, we speak faster than in the past and we make fewer stops between every spoken word (Polla-Mattiot, 2017).

Noise pollution negatively affects animals too. The noise of human activities endangers wild animals and affects their usual behavior in their natural habitat. It can damage their auditory system, which is more sensible and vulnerable than that of humans. For example, cetaceans become disoriented and confused, which causes them to beach themselves, as was the case for a shoal of giant squid found on the Spanish coast. Noise produced by human geophysical activity damaged their sensory organs and they became disoriented.

Noise produces not only physical damage but also stress and reproductive disorders. It can also influence wildlife's natural capacity to adapt. The noise of human activity can impede animals' ability to hear important sound that allows them to orientate, find food, defend their territory, avoid predators, attract a partner, and join a social group.

A study published in the journal *Science* (Buxton et al., 2017) demonstrates these negative effects. The first large-scale study on this topic considered 492 protected areas in the United States with natural resources in 14% of their territory. Scientists from Colorado State University and the U.S. National Park Service report that the noise being produced by humans' daily activity spreads wide and far, doubling the background noise in 63% of the protected areas and multiplying it by 10 in 21% of these areas.

A study on titmouses by University of Leiden researchers (Halfwerk et al., 2011) shows that noise pollution, by modifying the soundscape, pushes male birds to tweet in higher tones, greatly reducing the length of their pauses and thereby rendering them less attractive to female birds, which prefer birdsong in lower tones.

To attract partners and defend their territories, urban robins sing at night, when traffic noise decreases.

At the same time, there is a growing number of movements in defense of the sensory landscape of the countryside. The mayor of Gajac, a small town southeast of Bordeaux, asked French parliamentarians to declare as national heritage treasures countryside noises, such as the crowing of roosters, the ringing of church bells, the mooing of cows, the braying of donkeys, the chirping of birds, etc.[12]

Weintrobe (2013a) warns us against TV programs about nature in which the volume of the music and sound is so high that it obscures any interest in nature, including its sounds and silences. These programs do not provide any authentic information about other species, rather, they employ an anthropocentric point of view that does not consider nature.

Clinical vignette – let us stop shouting

Franca is a 23-year-old student from a traditional Italian family: her mother is a housewife and her father is a civil servant. She has three little brothers. Franca lives in an apartment invaded by the sounds coming from the television her mother leaves on all day long while she deals with housework, her brother's cries, and her mother's screams, as she tries to drown out her son's voices.

Franca tells me that living at home is hell: all that noise gives her headaches and forces her to wear earplugs. When she tries to make herself heard, nobody can really hear her, so much so that she has given up trying to express her point of view.

In the consulting room, when she begins to speak of her repressed and inhibited sexuality, she does so in a feeble and subtle voice, a sort of whisper. I must move close to her from my armchair to the couch, I must stretch my neck and twist my head to hear her. It is as if I were trying to absurdly enlarge my ear cavities. She forces me to move close to her, to make further attempts to understand those words that she cannot pronounce loudly. By making it difficult for me to hear her clearly, she projects onto me her fear of not being heard. This absolute need to be heard without any annoying background noise and sounds is associated with her narcissistic tendency to put me in the position of having to move closer to her to hear her words.

The fact that her whispering forces me to modify my posture in the armchair helps me to understand how much Franca desires that I be truly able to understand her, to listen to her with sensitivity and respect and that, as an attentive mother, I identify her childhood needs without any effort from her to make me feel them. I must feel at the counter-transference level her need for privacy and her need for me to receive however faint a message she sends me. In other words, she makes me feel her experience of not being heard. It is a communication that can be expressed only through an acting out and not a narcissistic attitude, a punitive attack. I favor her need to be understood, thanks to the possibilities of that environmental condition that Elizabeth Danze (2005) defines as the "acoustic intimacy" of the analytic setting.

Lucia Monterosa (2013) likens analysts staying immobile so they can discern an analysand's feeble voice, not moving to avoid any noise so they can hear, to a mother leaning over the cradle to make sure her baby is breathing. She points out that there are not only feeble voices but also voices protesting and declaiming in a penetrating way, voices that seem like foreign bodies and other voices that are inexpressive and hammering away. All these different sounds require acceptance and attuning, a sort of physical adaptation to something that the body of the other expresses to us.

Many families often leave the television on all day long. The family members watch television images only occasionally and absentmindedly. But sounds are the soundtrack of incommunicability, misunderstanding, and confusion. They fill an existential void and cover up the absence of affective exchanges among family members.

The communicative void directly and frequently influences those who stay at home, performing repetitive and frustrating work, more often the woman. The absence of two-way communication and the passivity toward noisy television messages can indirectly become a model of interrelationships, or, more precisely, a model of lack of interrelationships – a series of unilateral transactions in which everything is absorbed but nothing is actually gained. From the beginning, children learn to co-exist with the television, a foreign third party, which can compromise their attention, concentration, and communication skills.

In some experiences of observation of newborns and young children, in whose group discussion I had the opportunity to participate, the observer reported to have noticed strong correlations between the television being perpetually switched on at high volume throughout the visit, even if no one watched or seemed to listen, and the passivity of the child. The child went from unsuccessful attempts to attract maternal attention in any way possible, to apparently self-healing, substantially autistic attitudes, such as shifting his attention toward repetitive and monotonous games, in an attempt to soothe loneliness and to face the disappointment caused by the lack of maternal response, positive or negative, to his requests.

When the family is at the dinner table, it is common for the father to ask everybody to be quiet so that he can enjoy the evening news in peace and quiet. The news on television assumes the sacredness of a rite that is repeated every day. This deprives the act of being together at the table of every ritual and communicative value. The pleasure of conviviality is relinquished and the satisfaction of the children's need of attention is denied. Driven by the lack of the father's response to their needs, the children are virtually obliged to direct their attention and curiosity to the all-powerful television or to a videogame at their fingers.

All is homologated in a discursive circularity without relevance, where everything becomes equivalent and remains indifferent in a continuous and interminable stream of meaningless or, at least, interchangeable stimuli. A special and peculiar form of violence is created – the opacity of indifference, the product of getting used to repetitive, serial, and multiplied images and sounds (Schinaia, 2019b).

Reported clinical experience highlights how necessary it is to avoid acoustic disorder to allow childhood needs to find listening that is not concentrated or distracted, but a freely floating listening, dream similar to the maternal reverie described by Bion.

In his *Horror Pleni. La (In)Civiltà del rumore* (Horror pleni. The (de)civilization of noise) (2008), Gillo Dorfles wishes for the advent of a *horror pleni* (horror of what is full). He encourages today's women and men to express their proper autonomous individuality, re-establishing between them and their neighbors between their generation and the next, between daily actions and artistic creations a "stop between." Without such a "stop between," humankind risks succumbing to the horror of a "full" that cannot be fragmented and controlled and instead is dominated by the unstoppable flood of sounds, buzzes, and dins of "full" noise.

The conductor Teodor Currentzis argues that music cannot be read in the notes but between the notes. For him, music is not the black of a page but the white; it is the silence that descends like the night (Videtti, 2019).

The search for a place where Franca could be listened to without shouting, where she could share her suffering silences, a place not polluted by dissonant and cacophonic voices and annoying and harmful sounds, makes me think that human beings can express the same creative trust as Franca and build a world that can communicate without deafening sound, a world in which all of us can live in a positive manner without any damaging background noise.

Notes

1 Light pollution no longer affects only urban areas, but has come to touch most of nature. In a 2020 study, Jo Garrett and her colleagues at the University of Exeter (UK), along with BirdLife International, show that 51.5% of key biodiversity areas never have completely dark skies. The only areas where nights remain dark are Antarctica and marine protected areas. Dark sky parks, protected areas of the highest quality of night environment, have been recently created. In Italy, San Vigilio di Marebbe in South Tyrol is awaiting official certification as a dark sky park.

2 In *Darkness: A Cultural History* (2018), Nina Edwards criticizes the neat division between Western and Eastern culture because in both cultures literature, music and visual arts are fascinated by darkness. She notes that the Japanese word for "Japan" (Nippon or Nihon) means "origin of the sun."

3 The expression comes from the marked use of dark, earthy colors and the presence of black backgrounds, shadows and contours. Goya painted these 14 pictures, likely between 1819 and 1823, on the walls of the house in which he lived late in life. Although some art critics doubt their authenticity, they are now displayed in room 67 of the Prado Museum in Madrid.
4 Some interpret narrator Charles Marlow's journey through the jungle as a metaphor for the discovery of the unconscious.
5 In her novel *Voyage in the Dark* (1934), in which the main character lives in the Antilles until 16 and then moves to England, the writer Jean Rhys expresses an opposing point of view from that of Conrad. In fact, in this novel, England, and not the jungle of Marlow, is defined as an inhospitable, sad and dark place where everything (the colors, smells, flowers, people, and even the moon) is different and flat.
6 The monastery was constructed over the grotto where Benedict of Nursia, the founder of the Benedictine Order, stayed 1,500 years ago, as his biographer Pope Gregory I reports (Boatti, 2012).
7 If you search for the light, Benedict, why have you chosen this grotto?
   No grotto can have the light you seek.
   But you continue to look for the ray of dark
   Because the stars shine only in the dark.
8 In recent decades we have witnessed such an increase in the number of visual images that our lives seem to be saturated by them. From Google to Instagram, from videogames to visual art installations, this transformation is producing a global society that generates confusion. It simultaneously liberates and disturbs: we not only see the world, but we continually reproduce it in images, which we share and exchange with other people. Our first attempt to understand reality is now visual. So, too, are our attempts to modify reality entrenched in this new visual culture (Mirzoeff, 2015).
9 The retina's peripheral cells determine our perception of the dark. Once freed from the absence of light, they activate and produce that peculiar vision we name darkness. Thus, perceiving darkness is neither an inability nor an incapacity, but an action.
10 The term inspires the title of Grotstein's 2007 book *A Beam of Intense Darkness: Wilfred Bion's Legacy to Psychoanalysis*.
11 http://www.parlaritaliano.it/index.php/en/projects/44-clips-corpora-e-lessici-.
12 www.telegraph.co.uk/news/2019/05/24/french-mayor-seeks-heritage-status-sounds-countryside-residents.

Chapter 8

From the individual to the social sphere

Freud (1924) notes that few people can tolerate reality without misrepresenting or manipulating it.

Thomas S. Eliot (1936) writes that humankind cannot bear too much reality. We can withstand reality only if we conceive it as a purely chronological sequence of past, present, and future events. The other reality that reality that might have been is only an abstraction of a perpetual possibility in a world of speculation.

Bion (1978) validates the concept when he points out that fear of dealing with the truth can be so much that doses of truth are lethal.

Ghosh (2016) and Foer (2019) agree that it is no coincidence that great literature has never seriously considered and even ignored the topic of environmental disasters.

The same defense mechanisms we find in individual patients, such as confusion, obsession, denial, projection, externalization, splitting, and dissociation, can be found and described mutatis mutandis in groups and communities.

Further evidence that refusal and denial are not limited to individual defenses but also apply to group ones comes from a social psychological study by Susanne Stoll-Kleemann, Tim O'Riordan, and Carlo C. Jaeger (2001) in which defenses such as refusal and denial are recognized as responses to wide socio-cultural fears and anxieties. People may report anxiety and fear about climate change, but resent or deny what they cannot accept as a justifiable change in their behavior, for example, taking mass transit, riding a bicycle in the rain, or investing in expensive home insulation.

Indifference, absentmindedness, laziness, trivialization, devaluation of scientific reports, underestimation of catastrophic consequences, and apathy toward the involution of the relationship between man and nature can be interpreted as defenses against an unbearable anxiety. This anxiety is even made more acute by the social networks, which do not allow a careful preliminary evaluation due to a hierarchy of information. Thus, the outcome is a public opinion superficially excited and not correctly informed due to the prevalence of emotionality frightened by alarmism on the primacy of

DOI: 10.4324/9781003220077-9

reasoning and reflection. They make us search for more visible enemies, enemies whose presence does not require us to radically change our lifestyle. Examples include manipulation, conspiracy, the deceptions of the hidden power centers, the invasion of migrants, terrorism,[1] other people, or distant countries with uncontrolled economic development, such as China and India.

Searles (1972) translates in group terms what was discovered in his consulting room at the individual level. He postulates a double link with the biosphere, characterized, on the one hand, by an adult matching relationship with our eco-systemic container that helps us to recognize the environmental crisis and deal with it with maturity and, on the other, by a pathological symbiosis with the environmental crisis that dehumanizes us and that literally attacks our nature and that of future generations (Magnenat, 2019b).

The illusion of control must be classified among group defenses because when we underestimate environmental risk, we do not do it because of indifference or cynicism but because we believe that these phenomena are, or at least can be, under our control, even if an accurate assessment shows that this is not the case. Ancient Greeks had a specific word and even a semi-divine personification to designate our inability to see danger: Atë, the goddess of ruin, deception, and foolishness, a minor figure in Greek mythology who makes humans lose their sense of proportion, instigates them to arrogance (hybris), and leads them to perdition.

In *Men in Dark Times* (1968) Hannah Arendt focuses on another phenomenon, a defensive modality opposite to manic acting, that is, the exclusive focus on ourselves, the contemplative dimension, the withdrawal and taking refuge in our interiority, which she defines as "inner emigration." It is when people face an apparently unbearable reality and, to do so, shift from the world and its public spaces to an interior life or simply ignore this world in favor of a world of imagination, an "as it ought to be" or "as it once upon a time had been" world.

Many reflections on defense mechanisms about war and specifically nuclear danger can be applied today to climate change and generally to environmental damage.

Hostile and destructive impulses are part of a person's paranoid disposition (Storr, 1972).

Franco Fornari (1964) writes some of the thought-provoking pages on the psychoanalysis of atomic war, arguing that it is the result of the paranoid work of mourning. A normal person needs to be involved both in the guilt and responsibility of a possible destruction of all mankind: he unconsciously feels guilty but denies this feeling or projects it onto others, who consider the only ones who are responsible for the disaster. A widespread sense of individual responsibility and a push for change could only come from the recognition of the sense of guilt, considered and used as a sign that we can kill others (Fornari, 1966).

For Hanna Segal (1987), every war activates regression from the depressive position, as well as mobilization of paranoid–schizoid mechanisms, splitting, and projection. But the existence of nuclear weapons means something more, that is, the activation of more powerful defense mechanisms because of the threat of total annihilation.[2]

David Bell (2015) describes the role of the death drive in different models of the contemporary Kleinian theory by referring to a part of a dream of a patient in which there had been a nuclear explosion, dust and fallout fell all over him, yet all was pleasant and peaceful. Each model focuses on different features of this dream in its interpretation: one model can focus more on the pure and immediate pleasure of destruction (the explosion); another on the seductive flattery leading to a sort of indifference or passivity (the dust and radioactive material falling over the patient); another on the sadistic pleasure of having maintained the object in a peculiar state of half-life (the feeling of pleasantness and peace).

Similarities exist between Hannah Segal's explanatory model (and, in my opinion, Franco Fornari's) about nuclear danger and the model that can be applied to climate-change dangers in schizoid–paranoid and unconscious destruction, according to Michael Rustin (2013).

Events such as large-scale catastrophes and their anxious experience of ruin, war, nuclear war, natural disasters, and epidemics can become part of the set in which oneiric experiences of mental precariousness, elimination of existential projects, depression and anguish of death, fear of the future, interruption of significant emotional relationships, bereavements, and irreparable losses are represented.

The indelible images of environmental disasters that the media continually broadcast can round out this oneiric scenario, which has personal and individual origins and can also be influenced by societal factors such as images. In dreams, a person can use images of the consequences of environmental disasters as a tool to visualize the darker, less integrated aspects of his personality. An external image, for example, one representing a "disaster panorama" at the iconic level, can assume an organizing function in the dream. It facilitates the detailed and organized representation of a set of disorganized internal images in search of representative aggregation.

George Marshall (2005) connects our defensive response toward climate change with our anxieties about mortality. Similar to the experience of death, the experience of climate change confronts us with a permanent and irreversible loss. Marshall says that every time he looks out of his window, he thinks that the world we experience is only a passing dream and, if we do not try to stop this disaster, the world will never exist again except in fading memories or photographs. This mirrors his thoughts about his own death.

Clive Hamilton (2010) considers Marshall's observations and connects the difficulty of becoming aware of elemental change to the planet that occurs over decades or even centuries with the Freudian difficulty to conceive death, both ours and that of the people closest to us. He hopes that, after denial, there can be a state of depression, a state difficult to reach because Earth dies much slower than human beings. After depression, the work of mourning is necessary and that involves becoming aware of and accepting new living conditions. This does not mean saving the world as it is now: it means to think of a new world starting from present difficulties.

Lertzman (2015) introduces the notion of "environmental melancholia"[3] to describe the condition of unworked mourning about the effects of climate emergency: even those who care about ecosystems and future generations are paralyzed when they must translate this worry into concrete action.

It is not a matter of apathy (lack of pathos), emotional inertness, or awareness: it is the fact that feeling too intensely about the problem appears to lead to a sort of paralysis and a sensation of being unable to act. When we deal with the climate issue, it is difficult to individuate the object of the work of mourning and thus more difficult than, for example, mourning the loss of a person. So, too, we must overcome cultural barriers that hamper our ability to become aware of the situation. In fact, the work of mourning is about non-fully understood and interiorized loss. The temporal dimension of the climate crisis is another psychological challenge. We suffer not only for a loss that has not occurred yet, but climate change occurs in slow motion, metaphorically speaking, too slowly to alert our attention. This is a chronically hazy state of things that makes us prone to assimilate only information that confirms our beliefs.

As a starting point, we should recognize our collective suffering and ambivalence toward climate change. According to Freud (1917), mourning is a process toward awareness and not a hindrance. Thus, we should make a work of mourning our dreams and illusions and listen to our many, often contradictory emotions. A psychological work on these topics in ourselves and in our relationships with others would allow us to be freer and able to act positively.

Lerztman is against the so-called "myth of apathy," the emotional obstruction and affective anesthesia on which many environmentalist campaigns focus and according to which people do not act because they do not care. Actually, worry is not only present; at times, it is excessively present and connected to complex unconscious defenses. We must stop worrying and thinking of our finitude in relation to an environment assumed as unchangeable and unbreakable. Rather, we ought to worry about the risk of disappearing along with the environment because of our behavior.

To have an authentic relationship with a dynamic and uncertain world, it is crucial to integrate and not avoid our ambivalence and anxious feelings of loss. Magnenat (2019c) points out that the experiences in early relationships are constituted by successes and failures in communication and by development or interruption of thought. We carry inside of us the traces of "our fundamental duality," remnants of experiences that infiltrate both "the non-psychotic part of our personality" (characterized by realism, creativity, and mentalization), which he calls "sapiens," and "the psychotic part of our personality" (characterized by a detachment from reality, narcissism, destructiveness, and de-mentalization), which he calls "demens." These experiences reappear every time a rapid mutation of the historical phases of a culture occurs, when those who guarantee the bearing and framing structures of our societies desist or disappear, as it has been happening, with humankind detaching from its environment and plunging it into crisis. Anxiety over the extinction of our species as well as the faith in our future could be nothing more than collective contemporary symptoms of a transitional state in our civilization, a state that might allow us to acquire an individual Ego and a cultural Super-Ego driven by ecological values.

Environmentalism without any ifs or buts as a defense

The environmental movement has clear historical merits in the fight to preserve, reduce, and repair ecological damage. That said, we must discuss some contradictory features in the movement's history and ideology so as to avoid committing errors of evaluation and communication that reduce the strength of the environmental message.

Conformist and fanatic adherence to the environmental ideology can mark a retreat toward the fear to feel, think, and compare oneself with others. As such, although this adherence is a defense mechanism that seems to idealistically value human relationship with nature, in fact, it minimizes it. This occurs when we render the relationship rhetorical and substantially uninteresting. Those who are beset by a nostalgic desire to return to an imaginary past and consider all the changes that progress brought as elements of destruction of a happy and idyllic past are nothing less than reactionaries (Lilla, 2016).

We must pay a lot of attention to the so-called conservative point of view of the notion of nature and be suspicious of the naturalistic fundamentalism. This is because it is a historical fact that the interpretation of the notion of nature and of what is natural has had an ambivalent status. On the one hand, the notion of natural rights, which later became human rights, meant equal conditions for all against every ethnical and racial prejudice. On the other hand, the notion of nature was used to legitimize religious and political power through the repression of acts and practices that, all along different historical periods, had been defined as "against nature" (Esposito, 2020). If the notion of nature is built as the opposite of what is judged as artificial and artifact, in this sense, this notion can exclude as abnormal and regrettable everything that does not satisfy an alleged normativity (Chiffoleau and Thomas, 2020).

A critical praise of the natural world, in which, by paraphrasing Voltaire's (1759) *Candide*, everything would work for the best in the best of the possible worlds, obsessive dramatization of environmental defense mechanisms, a continued use of alarmist tones and apocalyptic interpretations, opposition to scientific progress, can all promote processes of magmatic fusion, substitution of the symbolization processes, and identification with a group mentality in basic assumption of the support of hallucinosis and idealizations (Malidelis, 2019).

The "Nature" of ecological ideology is a late construction of culture, not the rediscovery of a basic authentic state (André, 2020).

Slavoj Žižek (1992) warns against the "ecology of fear," a form of compulsive activism that can be called "Super-Egoic environmentalist moralism." Such attitudes are counter-productive because they foster rigid and extreme anxiety, the prelude to desperation and panic. Climate terrorism, for example, can promote the emergence of persecutory and primitive anxieties and even the activation of psychotic defenses.

Mireille Fognini (2020) denounces as politically opportunist the activism of some groups that she defines as "ecologarchies" (ecological oligarchies) harmful to scientific ecology. Thus, she stresses that the exaggerations of a doctrinaire and indoctrinating proselytism, if not sectarian, under the aegis of an intense and radical green activism, have provoked contradictory passionate reactions, reinforcing splittings and feelings of subjective impotence.

For Ambrosiano and Gaburri (2013), identificatory self-satisfaction can take on a non-individuated, mass social dimension. This can find expression even in an apparent anti-conformism. Every ideology, even the most vital and with the best of intentions, such environmentalism, can embrace the fanatical and impetuous.

The Intergovernmental Panel on Climate Change recently commissioned Climate Outreach to produce "Principles for effective communication and public engagement on climate change," an evidence-based communications handbook for the panel's writers. These principles consider both the intrinsic uncertainty of climatology and the fact that values and social rules strongly influence the way through which environmental information is experienced and translated in manifest behaviors.

In spite of the urgency of the discussion on the consequence of our alimentary styles, this discussion risks being halted by a confrontational fanaticism that produces nothing but fury and hurt. Some vegans staunchly defend animal rights and anti-speciesism and, because of the unquestionable value of their alimentary choices, often use integralistic tones to appeal to psychological terrorism. On the other side are those omnivores who, feeling themselves unjustly criminalized by fanatical vegans, display a superficial and indifferent sarcasm that does not recognize the ethical value of vegan convictions (Niola, 2020).

Each of us needs to be protected in our current environmental situation, characterized by so much destruction of so many kinds, in so many places, affecting so many people and other creatures, with no end in sight. It is no surprise that environmental activists complain about the diffuse apathy that meets their efforts to arouse concern (Nicholsen, 2002).

Recognizing the problem is strictly connected to the desperate impossibility of solving it. It is impossible to respond to the maniacal hope of repair through easy solutions (a hope followed by disillusion and the end of expectations if the solution does not arrive rapidly, in the desired and undeferrable time) with a mature and depressively working hope that skirts the childish "all and now." Rather, it is possible to respond with the nihilist and passive acceptance of damage without any hope of change, an acceptance that is a form of anxiety that can be called "eco-anxiety" and is strictly related to the experience of the inevitability of a catastrophe.

It must be added that efforts immediately directed to actions of environmental change can fail because they do not consider confused affective investments, memories, desires, and losses (Lertzman, 2015), elements that inform our environmental responses and produce a disparity between the level of awareness, worry, and evaluation capacity of our ideas about environmental damage, and the consequent actions and practices to be taken. These actions and practices require an amazing impulse to be taken but often are not based on conscious thought.

The environmental protest movement, whose leader is now Greta Thunberg, is necessary and praiseworthy and shakes the conscience. To be truly effective, it must be connected to the complexity of environmental issues and the actions to take, and consider all political, economic, scientific, social, and emotional aspects at play.

John Steiner (2018) explores the timeless dimension of idealized mental retreats by appealing to the so-called "Garden of Eden Illusion," where time stands still, everything is perfect and nothing can change, there is no development, frustration, loss, or passion. If the trauma of disillusion occurs too abruptly, or the suffering of waiting is too intense, defenses are mounted against the impact of reality. These defenses lead to a misrepresentation of the reality of life in which experiences that involve time are refused in favor of instant solutions based on omnipotent thought.

Loss and conflict spawn defensive movements, such as denial, distancing, and apathy. A good strategy could be to make us emotionally secure to create areas of dialogue and collaboration to reduce the intensity of our defenses, share our internal worlds, and connect with our creativity and capacity to mend. Creating conditions for participation, avoiding drastic judgment, reducing the space of the "environmental Super-Ego," fostering collaboration, improving the space of the "environmental Ego" so as to contain and regulate the effects of the environmental crisis – all are means to encourage people to explore their interior dilemmas and promote solicitude and creativity.

A politics able to face desperation, loss, and emotional paralysis is far more useful than a politics that blames, gives space to an apocalyptic terror regarding environmental change, or simply proposes a list of good and right practices for saving the planet, without considering how emotional difficulties hinder people from understanding and putting these practices into action.

In a speech he delivered in remembrance of victims of environmental disasters in the province of Belluno on March 12, 2019, Italian President Sergio Mattarella noted that, in the protection of land, lies the risk of maniacal attempts to adopt simplistic and insufficiently thought-out solutions. He stressed the necessity to learn from experience: without experience, containment and regimentation cannot deliver positive results. On the contrary, they can produce negative results that violate established protocols and disturb age-old balances that must be defended.

Split between good nature and bad nature

Weintrobe (2013c) reflects on the difficulty of recognizing our mental dependence on nature, the defense mechanisms of splitting and denial we use to control the unpleasant emotions and feelings this reality provokes, and the need to work through mourning before we creatively confront the changed environmental conditions in which we live. She proposes a distinction between genuine love and idealized love for nature, and the latter is based on splitting. In opposition to idealized love, genuine love considers nature not as pure in principle, that is, a pristine, original, and primordial space, but something limited and imperfect, as is our love for it.

The idea of a once-pristine Earth is a contemporary myth whereby a nature pure in principle is defiled by fatal progress foisted upon it by apathetic humans. A nature that transforms into an Erinys seeking to exact revenge for the wounds progress inflicted upon her is a typical fantasy fueled by our sense of guilt. From this fantasy springs the idea of nature as a regulatory agency that judges those detaching from a supposed a priori natural law as guilty of a crime against nature. The nature–culture and nature–progress relationship must be at the center of a debate that involves psychoanalysts in the search for a balance that can sidestep both nostalgic and reactionary appeals and thoughtless plans for the future. Very briefly, the debate must result in a transformation that benefits the environment.

Then, there is a consumerism of nature, the opposite of an authentic love of nature. Here, nature appears immaculate and untouched, sometimes wild and adventurous: it has become an idealized market product in all-inclusive vacation packages for tourists who do not want any surprises. This is an invasive artificialization of nature, an intrusive process that leads to protected, gated areas that prevent contact with the surrounding world and that forbid entry to indigenous populations.

A tourist is a person who leaves with a vague hope to find in another place what he has at home. Tourism has the taste of a convivial life still full of meaning. But today's tourist finds places modeled according to the principle of economic management, in which every spontaneity has been eradicated to convert what is real in terms of market economy and then rebuilt as a setting. In this dehumanized atmosphere, the tourist is imprisoned in a highly efficient and profitable organization and uses his free (actually very little) time, destroying with his presence what he had come to find (Christin, 2014).

Žižek (2007) reconsiders the expression used by Timothy Morton (2007) and defines "ecology without nature" that phenomenon through which we romantically venerate nature by making our own projections and alternating idealization and denigration.

We must tolerate our ambivalent feelings toward a nature that can give us both life and death. We must recognize our limitations, that is, the fact that we are limited in our transformative skills and that the planet cannot always tolerate our transformative interventions (Ambrosiano, 2016).

Many environmentalists simplistically distinguish the "good indigenous" who live in harmony with nature and the Western technological society that broke this virtuous, intimate link and led us to ecocide. This perspective does not consider how the great scientific and technological discoveries were fundamental for ameliorating life and interprets every innovation as a potential danger, a terra incognita, similar to what the ancient cartographers reported as hic sunt leones (here are lions), a warning signal forcing us to detach from what is known or familiar and inviting us to repetition. An old (and certainly more conservative than prudent) maxim is, "Better the devil you know than the devil you don't."

It is mandatory to create and develop a new bioethics for the future, by accepting the complexity of a global reality in which "good" and "bad" cannot be easily individuated and distinguished, rather than fantasizing of recreating the nostalgic certainty of a time and place in the past in which some groups of people lived in a sort of Eden in a natural harmony with a pure environment. This fantasy is nothing more than the result of our romantic idealizing projections.

Scaffai (2017) argues that we must avoid both a holistic confounding paradigm and a classical separative paradigm (that is, the dualism between res cogitans and res extensa Descartes championed). The former, very present in environmentalist thinking, places the human and the nonhuman on the same level without considering historical situations and contingencies; the latter legitimizes Cartesian control of the spirit over the material. Both paradigms are unsatisfactory for Scaffai, who proposes and defends a distinctive paradigm that transforms the distance between Ego and the external world into something positive. The inversion of roles and positions between subjects and objects, individual and context, human being and animal, throws into crisis the logic of control and dominion at the basis of the separative and dualist paradigm. It is illusory to imagine us as one with the universe, following a sort of nostalgic and regressive ideal of an idyllic nature, without considering distinctions and differences, sometimes substantial, that occurred for historical evolutionary reasons. This has led to soothing separations and dichotomies like new vs. old, present vs. future, clean vs. dirt, functional vs. non-functional.

Let us consider the passionate exhortation of Ulysses to his traveling companions to go beyond the Pillars of Hercules, the last frontier of the known world, to be followers of worth and knowledge (Dante, Hell, Canto XXVI, Verses 90–142).

We should interpret this exhortation as an invitation to work on integrating the irrepressible and courageous yearning toward knowledge and progress typical of human nature and the depressive (but also courageous) awareness of our limitations, that is, that worth and not only knowledge, which literary critics often do not consider.

Bateson's metaphor (1972) of the acrobat who remains suspended over the void and, to not fall down, needs the maximum freedom possible to move from an unstable position to another represents the emotional and existential condition of modern man. This condition is characterized not only by a conflicting alternation of defense mechanisms but also by slow and continuous processes of individual and group awareness and depressive recognition of the limits of progress and human condition itself.

In his posthumous notes published with the title *The End of the World* (La fine del mondo) in 1977, Ernesto De Martino uses a very thought-provoking expression: vital catastrophe.

Notes

1   Luigi Zoja (2017) reminds us that Islamic terrorism has not struck Italy in recent years, whereas there were more than 83,000 victims of bad air quality in 2012 alone.

2   The United States and Soviet Union ended the Cold War in 1987 with a treaty limiting the use of ground-launched ballistic and short- and medium-range cruise missiles with short and medium range. The main motivation was that nuclear war is unacceptable and has no winners. U.S. President Donald Trump canceled this treaty in 2019 and thus triggered the possibility of a new arms race instead of continuing toward the complete elimination of nuclear weapons. I think that we must reconsider Hannah Segal's reflections and try to avoid a new nuclear arms race.

3   *Environmental Melancholia* is the title of Lertzman's book. Between 2006 and 2007, she conducted articulated interviews on the affective dimensions of environmental degradation in people living in Green Bay, Wisconsin, a highly polluted place.

Chapter 9

Work–health balance conflict

I was born in Taranto, the Apulian city of the two seas, which had been the wonderful capital of Magna Graecia. Among the many memories of my childhood and adolescence, the seafood of Taranto has certainly a central place. In fact, it occurs in several episodes of my life, which my memory has indelibly fixed. When I was a child, after school ended each year, I spent my summer with my mother and brothers at Lido Venere (Venus beach) on the Ionian coast, north of Calabria. We took the bus, then continued by foot and crossed a small wooden bridge at the mouth of the small river Tara, whose name probably comes from Taras, the mythological founder of Taranto. Tara's cold waters separated the baths of Lido Venere from that of another beach called Pino Solitario (lonely pine) located on the opposite bank.

We saw the beach starting from the top, with golden sand dunes covered by white wild lilies, and then going down, after the rows of wooden cabins and the mills with roofs of reed, in a large shoreline ending in transparent sea water.

We as children used to stay in the water until our lips turned purple. But when the adults called for us to get out, before leaving the sea, we dug our hands in the sand and, without any effort we collected handfuls of cockles. After purging them of sand, my mother cooked them for dinner with tomato sauce to season spaghetti. When I got older, cockles were replaced by clams, which I went to collect where the sea was deepest, repeatedly diving underwater.

For a few years, I lived in the old town of Taranto. My grandmother ran a fishing shop near the seashore. The shop's walls emitted a characteristic scent of sea and rope. I used the little money she gave me to buy myself a handful of scallops. A street vendor opened them in front of me while I waited.

Every Sunday, my father brought home a basket full of oysters, which he skillfully opened for the whole family as a starter for lunch. When I turned 14, he announced with much seriousness that I was growing up and this meant that I should learn how to shuck oysters myself: the shucking of oysters was going to be a rite of passage in my family narrative.

DOI: 10.4324/9781003220077-10

After many years, I looked for that beach, but I did not find it. I asked myself if I was not seeking an idealized beach, a place in my mind, an image biased by the deceptive memory of someone who stayed away for a long time. Unfortunately, this was not the case. It was not a false memory: the beach where I used to play for many years had actually disappeared. I was embittered and angry. I took a look at the mouth of the Tara River and I realized that it had partially deviated and ran through waste and pollution. It now sat in a piece of land with dying pinewood, neither part of the city nor part of the country. It is not even an industrialized area. It is a dead and terrifying place.[1] It seemed to me that, in spite of the proximity of the port's industrial chimneys and cranes, the Tara was more degraded than polluted. The same was true for the beach; it almost disappeared because it was occupied by one of the structures realized for ILVA, the pier advancing into the sea for about 1,300 meters. The pier was built by placing on the sea floor concrete caissons filled with toxic waste from the steel industry. Especially during windy days, the pier became a malodorous landfill, as did the so-called ecological hills, between the steel complex and the Tamburi district, originally built to contain mineral dust.[2] The demise of the pier had led to the erosion of the beach.

In place of the golden dunes of my childhood, there was a residual beach, no longer clear and bright, but hard and mixed. Because of the carbon coke deposit, a sort of gray-blackish blanket covered everything. The sea turned darker with greenish tones. The posidonia oceanica, which reached the shore, had disappeared. The color of the surrounding streets was reddish because of the carbon coke dust accumulating on the edges of the roads and encrusting the guardrails. The iron residue came from Italsider, Italy's largest steel producer. The plant had been built in the 1960s, almost as I departed from Taranto to study medicine in Northern Italy, at the University of Pavia.

Goodbye, cockles and clams of my childhood! The water of Mar Piccolo (little sea),[3] the inland sea of Taranto, a bay where some of the best mussel and oyster farms were found, was polluted by dioxin because of natural water exchange problems. I had the same feelings of Pasolini (1975) when he described at the beginning of the sixties the disappearance of fireflies, due to air pollution, and of azure rivers and limpid canals, above all in the countryside.

Relatives and friends firmly advised me to stay away from seafood, especially the raw kind. Pollution destroyed my childhood memories, even the olfactory ones, and forced me to authentically face my ignorance of the transformations that had taken place.

Cesare Pavese (1950) asked himself how it was possible that at 40, and with all he had seen around the world, he still did not know what his country is. Like him, I could no longer understand what the places of my first part of my life were and had become.

According to Alberto Manguel (2007), we use to leave our home forcibly or by choice, as exiles and refugees, immigrants, travelers, or simply because we were attracted by other landscapes and civilizations. Even when we declare allegiance to a certain place, we seem to be always moving away from it. This is partly because of our nomad nature and partly because of the fluctuations of history: our geography is more grounded in a phantasmatic and mental landscape rather than a physical one. Home is always an imaginary place.

The landscape is the most trusted mirror of society, which creates, feeds, strengthens it, but can also destroy it, annihilating its collective memory and, basically, in a sort of suicidal impulse (Settis, 2013).

Goodbye scallops and goodbye oysters!

A brief history of the industrial area

The cornerstone of the state steel production plant Italsider was built in the early 1960s near the city, two steps away from the Tamburi district. In 1964, the first blast furnace was fired. In 1965, the inauguration took place. These were the years of development and economic boom, well represented in the processes of producing steel as described in Silvia Avallone's novel *Swimming to Elba* (2010).[4] In this novel, Avallone writes that metal is everywhere, in the process of birth. You could see cascades of steel and glistening cast iron and viscous light. It was like seeing torrents, rapids, rivers of molten metal coursing through the flow lines, into the ampules of the ladles and pouring into the tundishes to drain into the molds of furnaces and trains. Every time you look straight up, you could see greasy fumes and hear robotic sound merging murkily. Raw material was transformed all night and day long. Ores and coals arrived by sea. They were unloaded at the industrial port from huge freighters docked there. Fuel hurried along on overhead conveyor belts, midair highways and overpasses, running and traveling the endless miles from the docks to the coal towers and the coke oven and then headlong into the blast furnace.

In the 1980s, the steel industry was in crisis. In the 1990s, Italsider was sold to a private industrial group and took the name ILVA. The new private group adopted an assertive style toward employees and promised to guarantee the right to work to everyone to mask its use of workplace blackmail. In 2006, the toxic metal work in ILVA's Genoa plant was blocked after many trade union activities and public protests. The company merely moved that work to Taranto, increasing that plant's pollution levels. As an example, in 2008, 1,200 sheep contaminated with dioxin were killed and animals were forbidden from grazing within 20 kilometers of the plant. In 2018, ArcelorMittal S.A.,[5] a multinational steel manufacturing corporation, bought the Taranto plant. A year later, ArcelorMittal S.A. threatened to leave, cease all activity, and trigger unemployment. It is worth noting that this has been the largest steel plant in Europe: it initially employed 25,000 workers, and watered down to employing about 8,200 people.[6]

In my opinion, industry in Taranto is a white elephant and not, as someone rhetorically put it, a monument to modernity. In fact, because of its enormous dimensions, it had a traumatizing impact on land, which accelerated the urban sprawl: to build houses for workers moving to the countryside, Taranto underwent a messy, chaotic, and unbalanced urbanization.

Cristina Zagaria (2013) describes the industrial area in these terms: 15 million square meters, 2,000 kilometers of tracks, 50 kilometers of roads, 16 plants, 5 blast furnaces, and the E312, the tallest chimney in Europe. The core of the Taranto plant is the hot working area, with many coking plants and 256 furnaces and, as a consequence, their fumes and vapors. Finally, there are the mineral parks: 80 hectares – corresponding to more or less 100 soccer fields – full of coke, iron, and limestone. These parks disperse into the air 700 tons of poisonous dust every year.

Similar to Zagaria, Alessandro Leogrande (2018) describes the former Italsider land as an immense territory of 2,000 hectares, full of chimneys, cast iron accumulations, and storage areas: it occupies more space than does the city itself. It is a world apart, a city beyond the city.

Due to the emission of dioxin, beryllium, and polychlorinated biphenyls (among the most toxic and carcinogenic substances), steel production has been a source of devastating environmental pollution. It has led to an objective increase of disease related to environmental pollution, especially in children. For this reason, in 2010, Taranto's mayor issued an order prohibiting children in the Tamburi district from playing outdoors in green spaces. This district is just outside the walls of the industrial area. The walls of all the buildings are totally blackened, all the gardens lack green because the gases have dried out the trees. The increase in cancer deaths has reached twice the national average (Leogrande, 2018).

According to Daniela Spera, the so-called Taranto Erin Brokovich,[7] whose story is told by Zagaria (2013), Taranto has been slowly poisoned by industry, greed, ignorance, politicians' silence, the need to work, the dirty games of trade unions, and people's fear of reacting. Taranto's population has allowed this whole fiasco. The venom has had its effect and the dose has become lethal.

Pope Francis (2015) considers immense environmental disasters and their consequent social, cultural, and disruptive effects on entire communities such as Taranto. He envisions instead the city as an open, shared organism that respects both the environment and all the diverse needs of its population. We must also protect the common areas, visual landmarks, and urban landscapes that increase our sense of belonging, of having roots, of "feeling at home" within a city that contains and brings us together. It is crucial that the different parts of a city be integrated and that its residents enjoy a sense of the whole city, rather than being confined to a single district and failing to see the larger city as a space that they can share with others. Interventions that affect the urban landscape should take into account how different elements taken together can form a whole that is perceived by its inhabitants as a coherent and meaningful framework for their lives. For the Pope, cities that are full of spaces that connect, relate, and favor the recognition of others even in their architectural design are beautiful.

Between the past and the future

There are two Tarantos. The former is the city of nostalgic memory, how it was once upon a time, simultaneously maritime and agricultural, inhabited by shipyard and military workers, peasants, mussel farmers, breeders, and fishermen, but also by intellectuals firmly rooted in the local culture. The latter is the so-called post-ILVA Taranto, the city that must pay an unacceptable price for air pollution, a disturbance in its urban landscape and the absence of minimal conditions for an adequate level of health. Nonetheless, in post-ILVA Taranto, commerce and thus economic well-being increase: the individual and group standard of living has improved and most people no longer live in run-down homes. Most young people now have the opportunity to study.[8] This is a dilemma or an ambiguity that emerged when the steel industry came to the city: people had to choose between health or work, well-being or environmental degradation. This is the highly painful dilemma facing brutal current reality: ever-increasing pathology and death triggered by pollution.

Regarding this dilemma, there are two positions. The first is represented by the supporters of the right to work and thus of the maintenance of the steel industry. They espouse a new model of development based on remediating polluted soil and groundwater. In other words, they would radically change the present and bring about full environmental sustainability. The second position is represented by the supporters of the absolute right to health who, in a nostalgic and utopian manner, invoke the elimination of industry. They are uncompromising environmentalists who dream about the absolute potential of tourism in an area that, after remediation, would recover its original beauty.

Some years ago, I was invited to Taranto to present a book of mine on psychoanalysis and architecture. When I touched upon the issue of restoring and regenerating the old city, I set off a lively debate on Taranto and its relationship with industrialization and the living environment – a paradigmatic example of the contradictions of our times. Again, there were supporters of Taranto of memory and nostalgia and supporters of the present, actual Taranto, who call for responsible industrialization that brings economic well-being but also pathology and death.

The conflict between health and work, both fundamental values at the basis of the Constitution of the Italian Republic, is terribly distressing; I would say it is unacceptable. It is nonsense. People should not be forced to choose between health and work, between the right to economic well-being – under duress, through the blackmail of unemployment and misery – and the right to live in a beautiful and healthy setting. When people feel imperiled – when their economic well-being, livelihoods, homes, and the ability to feed themselves are questioned, even if those basic elements are guaranteed by an industry that pollutes their neighborhood and threatens their children's future – they end up supporting untenable positions or telling themselves the story that ingenious solutions could be found to reduce future damage. People endorse what they would strongly oppose in different emotional conditions and social contexts.

According to Weintrobe (2013b), our identities and statutes are closely related to our lifestyles. In consumerist societies, we are actively encouraged to express our sense of identity through material possessions and discouraged from considering anything that can cast doubt on such a sense of identity. We know very well that in giving up an unsustainable and consumerist lifestyle, we are threatening that part of our identity of which we are not completely aware but which we fight tooth and nail to preserve.

When we are traumatized or blackmailed, we are less able to think positively and to imagine alternatives. On the contrary, we tend much more toward resignation and away from free action. In these conditions, we can identify with the aggressor.[9] Another defense mechanism is apathy, an inability to experience any form of empathy.

In *If This Is a Man* (1947), Primo Levi describes the subjective experience in Nazi concentration camps in terms of apathy as an emotional–affective anesthesia or incapacity to despair. Humans in concentration camps had become objects for other people.

Between Genoa and Taranto

At the same time, in a different manner, I also experienced a painful conflict. In 2006, I was in Genoa, the city in which I lived and worked. The women's movement of Cornigliano, the area of west Genoa in which the ILVA steel plant was built with the support of all citizens, forced the plant to stop all hot steel activities because the pollution was causing serious mental and physical disease in the surrounding areas. The company simply transferred that dirty work to its Taranto plant. I felt hurt in my total personal identity, wounded inside, knowing that the same toxicity was now being blasted into the air and soil of my hometown and the lungs of its residents. I felt confused: I was breathing less polluted air in Genoa and I felt guilty because my relatives and friends in Taranto were breathing in whatever poison was no longer floating in Genoa's skies. The feeling of relief and satisfaction I shared with the Genoese people was in conflict with the pain I felt knowing that a company shifted the problem to a socially weaker geographic area with less bargaining power. I was suffering because, through a mental operation involving splitting, I could silence the unacceptability of that shift in a sort of abjuration of my origins.

My birth in Taranto, a city from the center of the gulf looks out at that portion of the Mediterranean Sea called the Ionian Sea, favored my arrival in Genoa, a seaside town superbly nestled on a large port with the privilege of being located at the center of a gulf watered by the Ligurian Sea. With many efforts and attempts to find a balance, I had been able to strongly preserve my roots and to have a creative comparison with a different place and culture without building a myth about my original identity in my mind. This complex mental operation necessitates engaging in the hard work of transformation that leads to detachment from certainties offered by an easy belonging to a cultural group and avoiding mechanisms of conformist and compensatory hyper-adaptation.

I accepted my emotional ambivalence, an ambivalence insuperable and prolific at the same time, and the mandatory negotiation at the relational and cultural level. Thus, I was able to coexist with a binary and not excessively conflictual identity. In spite of this, the transfer of the hot work to Taranto put painfully into question my dynamic and unstable balance. This forced me to start a historical–sentimental journey to the past, a revision of my roots, so that I felt the need to ensure that collective memory was respected and preserved, first of all inside of me. I was unable to give an exhausting answer at the level of reality and action to the condition of depressive suffering consequent to the demanding emotional conflict. I think that I was able to find a partial answer by actively supporting environmentalism, an anti-discriminatory and non-evacuative environmentalism, a non-harmful model of production, no matter where it is located.

I believe that environmentalism cannot be localistic, self-referential, affected by the not in my backyard (NIMBY) syndrome, unable to reflect on the connection between environmental, social, and worldwide questions, reactionary. Rather, it must have a broad scope, that is, be on a worldwide scale to prevent transferring the most dangerous industrial processes to parts of the world that are far easy to attack or, in essence, to blackmail.

Because of the peculiar nature of the entire steelmaking process, the answer cannot be solely to shut down production only to transfer the "dirty work" to China or India and in those countries in which the workers' lives have no value and where the absence of adequate environmental laws produce worse ecocides than those occurring in Taranto (Leogrande, 2018).

How psychoanalysis can help

Psychoanalysis cannot give packaged and consolatory answers to such complex problems, involving political, economic, and social ideas and decisions.

Instead, psychoanalysis can help us to reflect upon the questions that individuals and communities pose and thus to avoid simplistic and reassuring solutions.

Thanks to psychoanalysis, we know that perverse and destructive features of human nature can be found not only in criminals, bad people, or those who staunchly deny climate change but also inside all of us.

The search for truth and the need to harmonize the right to health and the right to work require immense effort not only at the political and social level but also at the emotional one. This is because we must grapple with doubts and uncertainties that provoke deep anxiety and all the consequent fears and sense of persecution that tend to increase in group experiences (Bion, 1961).

Bion (1962) describes three ways of dealing with anxiety. When anxiety is completely unbearable, it is evacuated through projective identification, which consists of attributing to someone else our mental states: it is an unconscious operation used by both individual selves and political entities. When anxiety can be better tolerated – when it is possible to think and pass the reality test – so, too, reality can be better tolerated. Today we are more likely to withstand minimal levels of tolerance, sometimes controlled through a sort of moral superiority followed by the search for someone to blame and punish, and not through a process involving knowledge. The ideological witch hunt is more remunerative at the emotional level than is the search for a painful truth, which requires a strong capacity to deal with uncertainty and depression. In this sense, we witness the formidable resurgence of ancient childish defenses such as repetition: considering what is familiar and already known makes us feel safer. Instead of assessing what is new with a new way of thinking or with new tools, we settle on ideologies, which are often polarized between catastrophe and complacency, sometimes going from one position to another rather quickly as we seek simple solutions, without respecting the complexity, partiality, and imperfection of the various possible solutions. No wonder it can be easy to accept conspiracy theories based on the splitting between the good and bad.

According to Leogrande, in the case of Southern Italy, we witness the return of the origin of evil located always outside and never inside our social and political arenas, a phenomenon not seen since the Bourbon dynasty. This increases addiction to the worst, the absence of self-criticism, a useless and querulous victimhood.

The victims' resentment[10] and the lack of recognition of the shared responsibility at the individual and group level are not the only factors that motivate opposition to the situation. In fact, they do not allow any relationship, but only a repetitive pattern, a compulsion to expose indefinitely to the same trauma. They maintain mental passivity without promoting any working through and any possibility of transformation of trauma (Ambrosiano, 2016).

We must consider Leogrande's (2018) intellectual heritage: we cannot accuse those who ask the dramatic environmental question of fostering de-industrialization and unemployment; at the same time, we cannot blame those who defend the right to livelihood. Both these extreme positions are based on the same pre-modern myth of the immutability of industrial work. A possible solution could be to ask, claim, and bring about a radical transformation of industrial areas and of the work relationships of industry, as well as a radical transformation of the relationship between industry and city.

This entails creating a transition to a new production system characterized by progressive de-carbonization and emancipation from the monoculture of steel production. Furthermore, this involves seeking a new economic paradigm that can connect well-being and growth, development, and sustainability, inclusion and livelihood, and collectivity and the individual. Transitioning to a new production system that results in cumulative de-carbonization and frees us from steel production necessitates a novel economic model that innovates, transforms, and revitalizes areas affected by the inevitable fossil deindustrialization. Such a model must synthesize personal health and economic health, of the group and the individual, in line with "integral ecology," with the right to health of those who work not as secondary, but primary, fundamental, and, therefore, unavoidable.

In her novel *Veleno* (Venom) (2013), Zagaria tells through the point of view of Daniela Spera various stories of men, women, and children hurt in body and soul by the virulence of pollution, their terrible social withdrawal and isolation resulting from the feeling that the exchange constituting the connective tissue of humankind has been lost. We hear the voices, incredulous and scared by the overbearing emergence of evil, we sense the feeling of complete and total annihilation, the discouragement, and the demoralization. We have all experienced impotence and vulnerability. We know how frail our defenses are in the face of the inacceptable truth of damage.

Under these circumstances, we could also verify how a resigned subordination to a sort of bad destiny has been transformed into a capacity to denounce and fight. At the beginning, this was permitted by the commitment of a handful of big and wacky heroes and then involved larger and larger groups of consciously organized people.

If we are to effect positive change, we must come to grips with those anxieties that are full of confusion, bewilderment, anger, resigned resentment, pain, and fear. Detecting our denial is the other side of our feeling unable to change the course of events, but also of our capacity to face our sense of guilt, feelings of shame, and difficulties with self-esteem. All these things are consequences of a myopic utilitarianism, the result of a criminal manipulation of the truth that made Taranto's workers and residents believe that what industry offered them was a good way of life. All these emotional movements produced mental splitting at individual and group levels. These splitting are about an industrial production that produced death but also great profit, highlighting the difficulty of integrating the representation of the object in articulated images.

The environmental melancholia described by Lertzman (2015) possesses an ambivalent dimension. In fact, anger can motivate people to mobilize against industry for the environmental damage it inflicts but, at the same time, they can feel conflicted and fear possible consequences such as job loss, social ostracism, and appearing ungrateful for the fruits of industry.

What is proposed on a conscious level – that environmental damage will render Taranto a ghost town on poisoned land in the near future – must consider an underlying and not fully declared individual and community drama: people and communities must realize that at the beginning there were individuals and communities with needs and satisfaction, but then they were betrayed and violated in their most intimate aspects because they were deprived of the chance to trust a stable and predictable world.

For the Ancient Greek philosophers, Psyche meant "refreshing breath." This concept can be found in the Jewish tradition, as stated in Genesis 2:7: "And the Eternal God formed man of the dust of the ground and breathed into his nostrils the breath of life; and man became a living soul." We can make our psyche ease our breathing, reduce its defense mechanisms, if the air we breathe is good and how we breathe is easy.

At first, Taranto had been hopeful and proud of modernization and of the ensuing economic tranquility emanating from it, but then, it found itself disappointed because of the project's complete failure. This was not only the failure of a company or a ruling class, but of an entire community, signaling the end of the utopia of modernization.

Antonella Granieri (2016) writes about a similar predicament in another community, that of Casale Monferrato in Piedmont. Casale Monferrato had been the capital of asbestos cement production in Italy. As was the case in Taranto, that industry provided the entire population's livelihood and identity. Throughout the years, the inhabitants' identity was structured around the idealization of a powerful mother-industry, feeding her sons with nourishing food. However, after some time, it became clear that this food was toxic, that it was, in fact, a poison that would harm those living in Casale Monferrato for a long time to come.

Mara Benadusi (2018) describes the emotional catastrophe in the areas of oil extraction in Sicily. On the one hand, she reports feelings of salvation with connotations of abundance, well-being, and nature's dominance, on the other, feelings of damnation due to the symbolic and imaginary dimensions connected to the disastrous culture of oil.

The collective experience of being victims created a truly group amalgam and set aside individual wealth and class differences. That is, a defensive group process based on homogenization and on the experience of being victims eventually allowed the people of Casale Monferrato to become aware of their collective need to protest. Granieri argues that, through a sort of mass identification, the regressive fusion had become the illusory substitute of the lost object. Thus, the individual Self had given way to an ideal group Self, which had moved between the feeling of being designed subjects and the feeling of being people particularly resistant to contagion, something that would have saved them from death.

Ambrosiano and Gaburri (2013) argue that people have to internally reach a balance between "narcissism," the search for their personal peculiarity, and "socialism," the search for connection with the others. They refer to Bion but also to the distinction proposed by Esposito (2008) between "*immunitas*," the need to be isolated and closed inside their own identity borders, and "*communitas*," the chance to deal with the fear of contagion when they meet the peculiarities of others. For Ambrosiano and Gaburri, "*immunitas*" and "*communitas*" are not antithetical. In fact, they point out that for Esposito, the search for immunity is a fundamental element of community because the bond can threaten identity. In this sense, it is necessary to keep alive the need to maintain our identity borders and, at the same time, to loosen them when necessary.

External help is essential if we are to properly deal with our destructive processes and promote the development of our Ego resources in support of the suffering parts of our Self. This does not belittle distrust toward life and toward its meaning. It is necessary to find meaning in our dramatic life events, but not an immediate and consolatory meaning, as this would be little consolation for those who seek it. Trying to give meaning to something unimaginable necessitates going through a group mental space characterized by a feeling of loss and mourning, even of disappearance. This group mental space permits us to preserve a feeling of uniqueness and freedom and is open to the construction of bonds of reciprocal recognition.

Fédida et al. (2007) point out that some people experience unacceptable suffering that seems to bring them beyond the limits of imagination. Knowing the horror does not mean to be empathic toward it, rather it provides the chance to know the way in which the horror destroys our representations. Our capacity of empathy and identification with others, of inferring others' mental states, indicates what occurs pertains to the human realm. This is because, even if we do not experience what the other experiences, we can recognize that the other really experiences it. Thus, even when we recognize what is experienced as extraneous, we recognize it as similar to us. The quality of similarity we attribute to others is provided by the extraneity others show us.

We think better together than alone, even if individual thinking and the responsibility emanating from it must always consider group thinking. From this assumption, the point of view and the support of a third subject – a subject having the right distance – are able to provide a historical perspective on the suffering. This allows the emergence of multiple narratives about somatic–psychical pain and extends beyond the objectivity of construction, as stressed by Freud in *Constructions in Analysis* (1937).

For mental preservation in highly critical conditions, Kaës (2013) proposes psychoanalytic group work because the group is an interface between the internal space and the social and cultural space. The psychoanalytic group allows people to realize that all of us bring to the table unthought collective heritages, heritages of destructive violence, war, traumatic cataclysms, and mass denials. The group allows us to face what cannot be managed or understood, what is without meaning, control, or comprehension.

According to Fédida et al. (2007), we cannot say what has taken place, but we can try to create a place for it. This place is psychotherapy.

The rediscovery of the plurality of various individual and group identities allows the rediscovery of the plural identity of Taranto and avoids any escape into a one-dimensional future.[11]

In his novel *La Dismissione* (The Dismantling) (2002), the Neapolitan writer Ermanno Rea writes about the closing of the ILVA plant in Bagnoli, a town near Naples. There has not been any mention of converting the industrial area and so it remains a waste land. He calls the abandoned vast landscape, with the ruins of the steel plant, "the big Ferropoli" (town of iron): it comprises about 2 million square meters of land, a bleak giant who vomits 20 million liters of poison into the sea per hour. Perhaps Ferropoli will be destroyed with dynamite or perhaps it will be filed for future memory under "industrial archeology:" once upon a time, there was the industry or, rather, THE INDUSTRY.

I really hope that the historical, political, and psychosocial conditions that created the destruction that occurred in Bagnoli will not be repeated in Taranto. I wish that Taranto would return the town described by Pasolini in his *The Long Road of Sand* (La lunga strada di sabbia) (1959). In this book, Pasolini remembers when he dreamt Taranto shining on two seas as a gigantic, shattered diamond. He argues that Taranto is the perfect town. Living there is similar to living inside a shell or an open oyster.

The historian Salvatore Romeo (2018) writes that Taranto does not need to substitute the old industrial monoculture with a new one, touristic or agricultural. Rather, it is necessary to think of the future through different lenses from those we inherited. Romeo exhorts us to piece together the fragments we have right under our eyes and in our collective consciousness: Taranto means rebuilding an industry, discovering a landscape, valuing a history.

To conclude this chapter with a heartfelt proposal, I want to quote the Latin inscription on the external border of the basin of the fountain known as Wind Rose at the center of Piazza Ebalia, which opens up to Taranto's seafront promenade:

> *Et quidem, cum fortiter adversa vela ventis* (Even with adverse winds we will bravely sail).

Notes

1 The main character of Alice Zeniter's novel *The Art of Losing*, Naïma is a third-generation immigrant born in France. She tells of her dismay in comparing the beautiful Algeria her grandparents and parents told her about and the trees full of plastic bags she sees the first time she arrives in Algeria.

2 In February 2019, the Carabinieri (the Italian *gendarmerie*) placed under preventive seizure of the so-called ecological hills, following an emergency measure issued by the prosecutor's office of Taranto. The ecological hills are an enormous illegal landfill with many tons of industrial waste containing highly toxic and carcinogenic substances. In 2021, the ownership and management of ILVA were sentenced to more than 20 years in prison for environmental crimes.

3 Mar Piccolo (little sea) is an inland sea north of Taranto. It is a semi-enclosed bay forming two inlets, one in the East and the other in the West. Both inlets are connected to the open sea, Mar Grande (great sea), by two channels touching the Old City, the natural channel of Porta Napoli, and the navigable artificial channel separating the Old City from the rest (and most extended part) of the city. The peninsulas of Punta Penna and Pizzone originally separated the two inlets of Mar Piccolo. In 1977, Punta Penna and Pizzone were connected to the Aldo Moro Bridge. The water of Mar Piccolo is sweetened by the water of many underwater springs called *citri*, which created the ideal hydrogeological habitat for cultivating mussels and oysters, and of the springs of rivers such as the Tara, Galeso, and Cervaro.

4 *Swimming to Elba* (2010) is a social novel that describes the working life of Piombino, very similar to that of Taranto. Piombino is a coastal city in Tuscany between two worlds, that of the steel mill and its blast furnace that destroys human beings, and that of the island of Elba, described as an inaccessible paradise. All that remains of the past splendor of the Lucchini factory, which in the 1960s employed more than 20,000 workers spread over four blast furnaces, is the "Afo4," oven number 4, and the 2,000 men working there, of whom the youngest are 16–17 years old, struggling with *"(…) the rolling mill that turns a billet of steel into a bundle of steel wires and rods with an exponential specific weight."* Avallone depicts the steelworks as one of the main characters, as an organism that not only strikes fear because of its dimensions and its devouring power, but also is fascinating because of the nocturnal spectacle it provides. It is an organism of transformation, a monster whose machines, that is, its guts, have a frenetically destructive rhythm.

5 ArcelorMittal S.A. acquired the plant through a public tendering process and promised to respect important safeguard clauses. Nonetheless, at the same time, it was granted impunity for environmental crimes for five years. This meant that, as soon as the factory resumed production at full capacity, pollution levels returned to maximum. In 2019, ArcelorMittal S.A. threatened to withdraw the contract after the Italian government abolished the immunity for environmental crimes previously granted.

6 ArcelorMittal S.A. employs 11,000 people in Italy.

7 Erin Brokovich was famously instrumental in successfully suing the Pacific Gas and Electric Company in 1993 for contaminating drinking water in Hinkley, California with hexavalent chromium for over 30 years. Pacific Gas and Electric had to pay the largest compensation in a direct-action lawsuit in U.S. history, $333 million. The story was told in the 2000 movie *Erin Brokovich*, directed by Steven Soderbergh, starring Julia Roberts.

8 It is important to note that many young people emigrate to Northern Italy or abroad.

9 Ferenczi (1932), Ferenczi and Dupont (1988), and Anna Freud (1936) define and develop the concept of identification with the aggressor. When the force of an authority is so impressive as to frighten, this condition of great fear leads the victim to automatically submit to the authority's will, to foresee and anticipate his desires, to blindly obey, to completely identify with him.

10 In a 2013 book, Concita De Gregorio tells the story of an ILVA worker who has put a marble plaque under his house inscribed with the sentence, "I put a curse on you!" That is the title of De Gregorio's book.

11 Set in a deindustrialized area in eastern France, Nicholas Mathieu's novel *The Children Who Came after Them* (2018) tells the story of a group of teens. He describes the abandoned factories in which various generations worked as deconsecrated churches of a religion that betrayed its followers.

Chapter 10

Servants of the future[1]

Eugene P. Odum (1983), one of the founders of modern ecology, reminds us that the term "ecology" was proposed by Ernest Haeckel in 1886 and comes from the Ancient Greek *oikos*, which means "house, home, environment." Thus, the term stresses the equivalence between dwelling and respecting nature. Instead, Karl Popper (1945) invites us to consider the world as a marvelous place that we can still improve and cultivate as gardeners. This is possible only by being modest as those expert gardeners who are aware that many of their attempts will fail.

In a spiritualistic tone, Jung (1961, pp. 225–226) writes:

> At times I feel as if I am spread out over the landscape and inside things, and am myself living in every tree, in the plashing of the waves, in the clouds and the animals that come and go, in the procession of the seasons. (…) I live in modest harmony with nature.

In a 1950 interview (in McGuire and Hull 1977), Jung insists on this point by arguing that every person should have his own plot of land so that his instincts can emerge again. Cultivating the land is crucial at the psychological level, and for Jung, there is no substitute for it. We all need to nourish our mind and soul, but it is impossible to do so in urban tenements with few green areas or blossoming trees. We need to be connection with nature. Jung defines himself as a nature lover who relishes growing his own potatoes. Thus, he declares that he is fully committed to the idea that human life should be rooted in earth and soil.

Nina Coltart (1993) reconsiders Jung's thoughts when she stresses that, in an ideal world, all psychotherapists would have a garden and that garden would serve as a source of emotional nourishment. Gardening is not only an activity allowing more freedom and sensorial readiness and a simple recreation for the mind: overall, it is a symbolic area of emotional survival in which the Self can restore and rest.

Vittorio Lingiardi (2017) harkens to Voltaire's *Candide* passionate conclusion: "*Il faut cultiver notre jardin*" (We must cultivate our garden) by pointing

DOI: 10.4324/9781003220077-11

out that, if everyone of us cultivates our garden, we will have "our garden," the garden of humankind, whose plants and fruits can benefit all. By applying an oxymoron, this is an enlightened utopia and something pragmatic. Voltaire's garden offers a possible space for psychoanalytic work.

Spending time in wild nature, or just in our back gardens, permits us to reconnect with the oneness of life (Rust, 2008).

Landscape philosopher Massimo Venturi Ferrioli (2019) sets forth the idea that a rich and fruitful garden is an unprecedented metaphor for saving the future and transforming the world into that place humankind itself desires. Humankind becomes aware of its existence and can reunite with nature. Overcoming the dichotomy between nature and culture can give rise to a better world. This entails going beyond an opposition paradigm and accepting a holistic perspective, a perspective full of relationships and references, in which each element is indissolubly connected with others.

Pia Pera's book *Al Giardino Non l'ho Ancora Detto* (I haven't told my garden yet) (2016) starts with Emily Dickinson's poem by the same title and tells how she decided to restore an abandoned farm she inherited not by opposing nature but following it. In this way, she heeded the lesson of the Japanese philosopher and botanist Masanobu Fukuoka, the main proponent of natural farming. Natural farming can be summarized in four principles: do not cultivate the soil; do not weed the soil by tillage; do not use fertilizers; do not apply herbicides.

Cultivating a domestic garden is a concrete everyday action that requires effort and perseverance. This simple action preserves the health of the environment and of those who live in it even if it produces a minimal quantity of healthy and uncontaminated products (Mercalli, 2016).

In *The Well Gardened Mind* (2020), Sue Stuart-Smith uses the garden metaphor instead of the computer metaphor to describe the brain. She considers some neuroscientific results showing the benefits of nature and gardening for our mental health, in particular, related to impaired patients. She also argues that the garden can bring us to reality in an era characterized by virtual words and fake acts.

Our biosphere is the meta-setting that contains and produces, whose stability should provide the nutritive, narcissistic identity basis of our personality and collectivity (Magnenat, 2019c). For many millennia, Earth has taken care of her children by giving them an abundance of what they needed: today, children must take care of their Mother Earth and realize that their habitat is senescent, similar to elderly parents.

We must listen to Nature's loud cry for help. At the same time, we must listen to the needs of people, species, and ecosystems – even those very far from us – and to the needs of future generations and to the preservation of common goods, such as air and oceans, whose existence depends on our lifestyles.

The art critic Giulia Bartrum interprets the figure in the work of the Expressionist painter Edvard Munch, *The Scream* (1893) as not actually screaming but widening her eyes, covering her ears, and opening her mouth to block out Nature's powerful and heartbreaking scream. This is supported by a note Munch himself left on the frame of the 1895 version of the painting[2] in which he says that he sensed an "infinite scream passing through nature." Munch refers to a memory he had when he was in Nice in 1892: while walking on the banks of a fjord near Oslo, he saw the sky turning red and an enormous wave from the sea advanced toward him. This memory inspired the Norwegian artist to paint *The Scream*, one of the symbols of the restlessness and despair of contemporary human beings.

Pope Francis (2015) assumes a realistic and pessimistic but not desperate attitude. This attitude is similar to Gramsci's appeal to the pessimism of the intellect and the optimism of the will. According to the Pope, we should hope that there is always a solution, that we can always redirect our steps, that we can always do something to solve problems. Nonetheless, we can acknowledge that the rapid pace of change and degradation has brought us to a breaking point. As examples, consider large-scale natural disasters and social and financial crises: we cannot analyze or explain the world's problems in isolation.

Although we must not forget that there is a concrete possibility that the planet is gradually becoming increasingly inhospitable because of environmental catastrophes, as the Doomsday Clock[3] warns us by being set to 1 minute and 40 seconds before midnight (the symbolic hour for the end of the world), we can be cautiously optimistic (Jamieson and Mancuso, 2017).

Max Weber (1919) argues that we could not attain the possible unless we make an attempt to attain the impossible.

This optimism is the emotional symbol of our capacity to dream of the main existential aspects of our life and to transform our dreams into concrete actions (Magnenat, 2019c).

Although there is little time to take efficacious action for the benefit of humankind, we must recognize that we are both the problem and the solution. In the age of Anthropocene, we must take charge of a new awareness and a new ethics and avoid dangerous rationalizations.

For Mancuso (2019), the discussion about the possible existence of life in Earth-like planets or, at least, other planets in which life can exist, is a sort of reassurance for the disasters we committed and are still committing. It means that, however it goes, even if we run out of resources on Earth, we will find another place to continue our life. Actually, the existence of real forms of life different from those living on Earth is subject to many different inquiries and not scientifically demonstrated; for this reason, it must be considered as a speculation or a hypothesis.

Therefore, let us try to overcome the external and, as psychoanalysts, internal impediments; let us try to create those conditions that can enhance the expression of care and concern toward the environment. Let us not be discouraged if some of these attempts fail!

Freud (1927a, p. 53) writes:

> We may insist as often as we like that man's intellect is powerless in comparison with his instinctual life, and we may be right in this. Nevertheless, there is something peculiar about this weakness. The voice of the intellect is a soft one, but it does not rest till it has gained a hearing. Finally, after a countless succession of rebuffs, it succeeds. This is one of the few points on which one may be optimistic about the future of mankind (...).

By following Freud, Kaës (2012) does not express nihilist pessimism and fatalistic inevitability, a position that risks having highly implausible results. He points out that we must have a critical approach to the crisis these changes provoked. Nonetheless, we must not be tempted to be influenced by pessimism, or to look at novelties as something a priori optimistic. We are like the unlucky awareness of Hegel, which sees the world crumbling while perceiving that something novel is being born.

For the poet Andrea Zanzotto (2013), culture starts and grows as a spontaneous expression of the present dialogue between humans and nature, a dialogue similar to the mutual and loving comprehension between a mother and her fetus. But for Zanzotto, this was partially an illusion: two realities do not try to grow together, rather one reality unilaterally tries to prevail over the other. It is not a true dialogue, but a sort of string of insults in a monologue or hallucination. Because for Zanzotto, poetry re-establishes the dialogue between human beings and nature, poetry must obstinately continue to create a space in which what is authentically human can flourish by keeping alive the memory of a time projected toward a future of hope.

Moreover, Michelangelo Pistoletto (in Gatti, 2019), one of the main representatives of the Italian Arte Povera (poor art),[4] describes the planting of trees in the shape of the infinity symbol in the main square of Assisi and attributes to the artist the task of a gardener of the planet, able to bring together beauty and attention to the environment.

We need poetry and art, but also knowledge of our internal world to create an authentic dialogue, that is, a balanced dialogue between the excesses of intellectualization and those of emotion.

Ecology needs psychoanalysis and psychoanalysis needs ecology. In fact, the context for defining the notion of health (mental health included) has reached a worldwide dimension today.

Luca Mercalli seeks to understand the meaning of unconscious mechanisms: he begins his book *Non c'è più Tempo* (We have no time left) (2018) with an analysis of Primo Levi's work and shows the mechanism of repression of uncomfortable truths. During the rise of Nazi and fascist dictatorships, comfortable and consoling attitudes and explanations were created to avoid facing these phenomena. Similarly, today we create pseudo-rationalizing alibis and comfort zones to avoid respecting the planet's physical limits before inexorable physical and natural laws restore a balance without our presence.

After having described the spread of cynicism and arrogance that trigger an indifferent attitude toward human rights and the salvation of the planet and the need to identify our pathological parts, Bollas (2018) writes that today, it is fundamental to be free to identify those anxieties pervading our culture to create a positive change.

> If we are to modify unconsciously destructive processes and avoid the catastrophes that go with blindness, there is an urgent need for a wider understanding of human psychology.
>
> (Bollas, 2018, p. xxvii)

Ghosh (2016) hopes that future generations will be able to transcend the isolation in which humankind was stuck at the time of its derangement and to rediscover their connection with other human beings.

All these authors propose a defense of nature as opposed to a defense from nature. This proposal is not ascetic, but it invites us to consider frugality, generosity, and humility, a term coming from the Latin "humus," which means "soil." There is only one step from *humus* to *homo.* As we can see, the etymology seems to go back to a common Indo-European ancestor: *humus, humanity, humility* (Caron, 2020).

Greta Thunberg et al. (2020) wrote that our limitations start to become clear. The infinite regains its contours. We cannot have it all and this is right. In moderation, there is a different and larger freedom.

At the end of *Invisible Cities* (Calvino 1972), Marco Polo said that the hell of living beings is not something that will occur in the future. If there is a hell, it is what is already here, what we construe by being together. There are two ways to escape it. The first is easy for many: accepting the hell and becoming such a part of it that you can no longer feel or perceive it. The second way is a risky one that requires constant vigilance and apprehension: it requires finding out who and what in this hell are not parts of the hell and making them endure and giving them space.

The latter would heal the wounds that we inflicted on the planet, it would maintain the places, repair the damages caused by time and human beings, reverse the opposition to the planned obsolescence of goods.

In writing about a non-experienced experience that is always experienced, Winnicott (1974, p. 105) highlights how:

> (...) the fear of the breakdown is the fear of a breakdown that has already been experienced. It is a fear of the original agony, which caused the defense organization (...). There are moments, according to my

experience, when a patient needs to be told that the breakdown, a fear of which destroys his or her life, has already been. (…) In other words, the patient must go on looking for the past detail, which is not yet experienced. This search takes the form of a looking for this detail in the future.

Bollas (2017) reconsiders Winnicott's position when he describes the known but non-thought: this is because the object can cast its shadow, but the child is unable to work through this relationship through language or mental representations.

Dodds (2011) proposes applying Winnicott and Bollas' ideas, which regard psychoanalysis at the individual level, to the relationship with those feelings of catastrophe that plague all individuals and groups today. Psychoanalysis can help people experience these feelings with a wider reflective awareness through symbolization.

We must not only intellectually synthesize new knowledge coming from environmental science but also imbue with meaning the brute emotions flowing from this knowledge (Magnenat, 2019c).

"Silence is the real crime" is the title of a famous paper by Hanna Segal (1987) in which she argues that it is absolutely necessary to denounce the risks posed by nuclear weapons. She argues that, during the sessions, it is fundamental to not collude with the patient's denial of the external situation and to avoid imposing her or his worries on the patient. Janine Puget and Leonardo Wender (1982) touch upon this topic when they write about overlapping worlds (mundos superpuestos), that of the patient and that of the analyst, both full of social contradictions and ideologies, so that we cannot refer to a neutral transference–countertransference dynamics, that is, a dynamics divorced from cultural references that they often share. Puget and Wender refer to the concept of *vinculo* (link), originally introduced by Enrique Pichon-Rivière (1971), which is based on the idea that internal and external reality are not in opposition but in a continuous dialectic relationship forming a spiral movement that determines our mental functioning. Thus, the concept of *vinculo* includes the internal reality, the external one, and an original third, composed of both the internal and external ones. Puget and Wender refer also to David Liberman's (1970–1972) concept of "meta-setting," that values our surrounding social, cultural, and economic environment.

In reference to Nazism, Riccardo Steiner (1989) posits that neutrality cannot be defended or adopted at all when a political situation puts into question the psychoanalytic tradition's founding values. In such a case, neutrality simply means collusion.

It is certainly true that there are exclusive ways of feeling anxieties related to the environment and its changes. But it is also true that they are not exclusively related to the subject: they can come from human and non-human environments. These are unprecedented anxieties, for which we are not really equipped (Desveaux, 2020).

Dennis Haseley (2019) submits that, as he listens and speaks to a patient, other forces press on both him and his patient. These forces are nothing but the changes in our climate and their conscious or unconscious registrations in our minds and personalities. He understands "culture" in a wide sense, as something that includes psychoanalytic knowledge and practice, the planes we catch, the taxi rides from the airport, the traffic, the buildings where we hold meetings, the construction we pass on the street, the lights, the commutes we make to our offices, our heating and air-conditioning systems, our food systems, distant wars, etc. For him, culture is based on fossil fuels, which surround us. We depend on fossil fuels' utility. All these things, and the cultural tropes supporting them, are entrenched in our material and mental existences, that is, in the manners we symbolize, our dreams, the adolescent rites of passage, our unconscious fantasies of power and desire. At both the conscious and unconscious level, we are influenced by their omnipresence.

To avoid ecological catastrophes caused by development without rules or memory (therefore, "cannibalistic development"), we must explore the individual dynamics and the underlying conflicts, as well as the dynamics and lifestyles that are acquired inside the family. Recognizing these dynamics is the starting point to modifying them and, as a consequence, the individual and family lifestyles and to allow that, in a revitalized dimension of fraternal reciprocity, every single sustainable action becomes creative, respectfully restorative, and part of a worldwide renewal. This renewal is possible through re-assuming individual responsibility, accepting the reality principle, and opposing the skepticism of those who think that the single individual is condemned to a sort of impotence, closed in a kind of suicidal environmental melancholy.

We did not need to believe Donald Trump when he would say, "We will build the wall." We knew that, when he opposed reducing climate change, he was the spokesman not only of the industrial, economic, and financial lobbies but also of our childish greed. In our everyday life, we build great imaginary walls to deal with our pain, while knowing that our thoughtless lifestyles imply violence and suffering. We precisely individuate each pain and suffering we feel so we can quickly protect ourselves from them by applying denial (Weintrobe, 2019).

According to Bateson (1972), therapists have a twofold duty: on the one hand, to create light inside of us and, on the other, to look for every sign of light in others and to try to strengthen everything we find in them to be wise.

Haseley (2019) poses the following question: how can we be witnesses with our blind spots and sometimes even complicit in our consulting rooms, with the avoidance of environmental melancholia and anxiety?

Press (2019) asks how analysts can be so indifferent to the environmental problem. That is surprising because they spend their time exploring the early relationships of the child of man with his or her environment in all its terms, narrowly and broadly.

I believe that questions like those proposed by Haseley and Press are critically important and constitute the starting point that psychoanalysts must adopt to be civically engaged, to take a defined and clear political position before the urgent need to preserve and take care of the world. Psychoanalysts must contribute to the development of an environmental ethics that defines our alimentary choices, the products we decide to buy, the way in which we build our homes and cities and in which we travel.

It is said that when Socrates' disciples wanted to buy him a new pair of sandals to replace his old ones as a form of gratitude to his free teachings, he refused and argued that he went to the market only to look at the goods displayed and to verify how many things he did not need.

Lao Tsu argues that the sage avoids excess, extravagance, and arrogance.

Similar to Socrates and Lao Tsu, psychoanalysts should be able to revitalize the capacity to think and dream of a better future, contribute to valuing a sense of proportion and balance and maintain a sufficiently good life. They must work toward giving space to creativity, love, and knowledge so as to contrast illusory and magical thinking, and consider with integrity and sincerity the unpleasant features of human existence (Schinaia, 2019b).

In an April 24, 1927 (Freud, 1927b, p. 359) telegram to his daughter Anna, who was traveling to Italy, Freud writes about an appeal he signed with 39 other Viennese intellectuals: *"The essence of intellect is above all freedom, which is now endangered and which we feel committed to protect. We will always be ready to struggle for greater humanity and to fight against inertia and atrophy."*

A similar position can be found in Thomas Mann's words on May 8, 1936 in Vienna, on the occasion of Freud's 80th birthday. He argues that in the future, Freud's work will be recognized as the foundation of a new anthropology and a novel structure, to which many stones are being brought up today. This structure will be the future dwelling of a better humanity.

Thus, we can accept Segal's warning about the risks of an environmental catastrophe and the need to study specific historical modalities at the individual and group level through which we defend ourselves.

Cornelius Castoriadis (2007) argues a new imaginary creation of unparalleled importance in the recent past is required. Such a creation must be able to place other values at the center of human life than the expansion of production and consumption. This is mandatory not only to avoid the definitive destruction of Earth's environment, but also, and above all, to get out of the mental and moral misery of contemporary human beings.

Bion (1990) asks how a human being with a human mentality and personality cannot be interested or not concerned with the future.

Ghosh concludes his 2016 essay with the hope that, from this dire situation, will be born a generation able to take better care of the world than previous generations have been. This new generation should be able to go beyond the isolation in which human beings have been entrapped and rediscover their connection with other human beings. I like to define this new generation as composed of people who have never known what it is to fight for change and constitute the party of the future that we must visit to consider a promise and not a threat. In her novel *Borgo Sud* (South Village) (2020), Donatella Di Pietrantonio argues that the impure air of the world cannot take away its beauty. Here, I want to refer to a letter that Eleonora Ruzza, a student at the arts high school Amedeo Modigliani in Padua, sent to Greta Thunberg and was published by the Italian newspaper La Repubblica on April 7, 2019. In this letter, Eleonora imagines life as a race in which the arrival is the result of all the efforts we have made. In an ideal world, a race should be a pleasant activity, functional for our goal, and respectful of those who will come after us. The wind should breeze through our hair. Our feet should gently step on the grass lawn that we traverse. Unfortunately, we are usually more interested in our triumph than in our arduous route, and we continue to run faster. We trample the lawn. And we are convinced that it is better to face the wind than sail with it. At the outset, the damage of our furious race is irrelevant. But, step by step, the grass stops growing and the air becomes grayer. As a consequence, after many years, Earth begins to give way and slowly disappears beneath us. And we find a ravine. No one can stop the mad rush of people convinced that the precipice in front of them is a marginal problem. For Eleonora, Greta not only notices the problem but decides to stop. She sits in front of the ravine and takes a breath. And the people who come after Greta see her and begin to understand. So, they also sit, one behind the other, staring at the chasm that hinders their path. Then, all of them get up and, instead of running again, pick up the fallen pieces of land and build a bridge. Building this bridge takes a long time, but it is their only lifeline before the abyss becomes too big. From now, let us stop all races; the bridge is fragile. But we can still make our way.

Eleonora's words give consistency and strength to the hope of the constitution of the party of the future.

I want to conclude this book by referring to the second principle (Ecological Integrity) of the Earth Charter of the non-governmental organization Earth Charter Initiative,[5] whose aim is to *"(…) inspire in all peoples a sense of global interdependence and shared responsibility for the well-being of the human family, the great community of life, and future generations:"*

- *Protect and restore the integrity of Earth's ecological systems, with special concern for biological diversity and the natural processes that sustain life*
- *Prevent harm as the best method of environmental protection and, when knowledge is limited, apply a precautionary approach*

- *Adopt patterns of production, consumption, and reproduction that safe-guard Earth's regenerative capacities, human rights, and community well-being*
- *Advance the study of ecological sustainability and promote the open exchange and wide application of the knowledge acquired.*

Notes

1 In 1874, as a Member of the UK Parliament, Arthur Atkinson concluded his maiden speech with the sentence: "For we are not masters of the present but servants of the future."
2 There are four versions of *The Scream* (original title: *Skrik*), the most famous of which (created in 1893 with oil, tempera, pastel, and crayon on cardboard, 36 in × 28.9 in) can be found in The National Gallery in Oslo.
3 An initiative by a group of scientists of the University of Chicago's journal *Bulletin of the Atomic Scientists* in 1947, the Doomsday Clock is a metaphorical measure of the threat of a hypothetical end of the world for humanity. The threat is quantified through a symbolic clock whose midnight indicates the end of the world with the preceding minutes representing the hypothetical distance from it. Originally, midnight represented atomic war. Since 2007, it has represented every event that can permanently damage humankind, for example, climate change.

   In 1947, the clock was set at seven minutes to midnight. It has been reset 21 times since then. On January 23, 2020, it was moved the closest to midnight since its inception in 1947, 1 minute and 40 seconds. Its most distant status to midnight was between 1991 (the signing of the Strategic Arms Reduction Treaty I treaty) and 1995, 17 minutes.
4 Arte Povera is an artistic movement created in contrast to traditional art. It rejects the techniques of traditional art in favor of "poor" materials such as soil, wood, iron, and rags, with an intent to evoke the original linguistic structure of contemporary society. Another feature of Arte Povera is how art is installed: an art installation is conceived as the place for the artwork–environment relationship. One of Pistoletto's most famous installations is the "Venus of the Rags," in which he tackles regeneration and compares the classical and tidy idea of the beauty of Venus by placing a statue of hers next to an untidy pile of rags.
5 earthcharter.org.

Afterword

Luca Mercalli, President of the Italian Meteorological Society

At last, a book on psychoanalysis and the environmental emergency! For decades, we who work in the field of environmental sciences (climatology, sustainability, natural risks, etc.) have been wondering about our mistakes. That is, we continue to sound alarms increasingly documented and confirmed by the rationality and precision of measures taken from the ground and satellites and by the convergence of various scenarios set on refined mathematical models, but everything is silent. There is no reaction to the scope of the enormity of the current crisis. Not only does nothing happen: in a sort of unreal silence, it appears that steps are taken backward.

Even if we talk a lot about the environment, the concrete sensitivity of people continues to decrease. Indifference and denial grow. Predatory economics continues to promote its dissipative and dangerous model. It is a paradox: the more symptoms become clear, the more they are ignored, hidden, denied. The more there is a need to act, to take personal and collective responsibility, the more alibis, justifications, loopholes, and delays are invented.

It is like what happens to smokers: in spite of incontrovertible medical evidence of the toxicity of smoking, the blunt warnings on cigarette packets seem to pass through smokers' brains without leaving any trace. Thus, smokers appear to choose to commit a slow suicide and, if aware of what is happening, shrug their shoulders and continue on their way to predicted diseases. Very few people agree to open their eyes and change their lifestyle. Very few people agree to make changes today for a better world tomorrow, especially for their children, grandchildren, and future generations.

In the face of so deep and dangerous a historic crisis, a crisis that could potentially lead to the extinction of our species (we have evolved in an environment that is suitable for us; now we are altering it so much that we will no longer be suitable to it and, as a consequence, we risk being wiped out), we would expect mass mobilization, an "unprecedented effort," as advocated by the United Nations. But nothing happens! Many people go straight to the abyss in an arrogant and even joyful way. Few people appear to be aware of the problem and seek salvation but cannot change the course of events.

Greta Thunberg is living proof of our failure: we are grateful to this blessed Swedish girl for her personal effort. But it is ridiculous that the entire species of *Homo sapiens* that has been warned for many years about the climate crises by the best international scientists, finds in an autistic adolescent not a symbol but a disclaimer, a strange phenomenon not to be taken seriously, to be treated with indifference.

The fight against fascism was conducted by charismatic, mature, and monumental leaders such as Winston Churchill, who promised "blood, toil, tears, and sweat" for victory. Now, in this crucial moment for the survival of all species on this planet, we deny science and relieve our conscience by looking to Greta for an improbable and miraculous solution.

Where are the great political leaders? Where are the great intellectuals? Where is mass mobilization? What have we done wrong in communicating this crisis, we who have been studying climate for decades? Have we been too catastrophic? Or too soft? Too optimistic or too pessimistic? Have we given too much or too little hope? Have we exaggerated with guilt and fear or have we not communicated enough?

In this book by Cosimo Schinaia, I understood something more about this complex problem. Perhaps we have not done anything wrong: the dynamics of refuting the problem was inevitable because, in our human minds and behaviors, there are so many fragilities and contradictions that so disruptive a truth would have been difficult to accept, no matter the form in which it was stated. Perhaps we were only wrong in not encouraging more forcefully cooperation between the medical and human sciences about 30 years ago to find more effective methods to promote awareness and prevention.

Through a rich collection of quotations and references from diverse scholars and writers, Schinaia defends and promotes his positions, that is, that humans are unable to acknowledge collective and long-term alarms. In a not-so-remote past, the denial mechanisms Schinaia clearly describes in his book often provided an individual protection so as not to become overwhelmed by anxiety and depression in a world full of danger and hardship but in which no mistake was irreversible at historical time on a geological scale. But, at present, our attitude is terribly unsuitable for defusing those gigantic natural forces created by our technology. This attitude will compromise the environment for millennia to come and condemn all future generations to live on a hostile planet.

Schinaia offers us a brilliant diagnosis of our behavioral difficulties related to environmental protection, difficulties affecting more or less the whole of humanity and often assuming evident pathological features, well-described through some very useful and effective clinical vignettes.

At first glance, the impression is that Schinaia's relentless diagnosis based not only on psychoanalysis but also on evolutionary, behavioral, and social psychology, set forth our condemnation: we will not be able to rapidly and effectively change; the self-destructive drives, that appear to us under the masks of progress, growth, and hedonism, are too entrenched and powerful to be assessed as pernicious. In other words, Schinaia's diagnosis does not seem to permit a correction and a transition toward a sustainable world, a transition that is nonetheless slower, more peaceful, more sober, and apparently less desirable than that of competition, speed, and unlimited power.

Thus, this transition appears highly improbable. However, an "environmentalist psychoanalysis" who can comprehend the deepest mechanisms of the human mind could represent one of the fewer options to consider to do something. It can foster a transformative effective process, leading to the greatest step in the history of humankind. This is because we have no more time.

Schinaia makes me understand that communicating such uncomfortable truths requires caution: they are strong strokes inflicted to the fragile and precarious constructions of the Ego. This is the reason why these truths are often strongly rejected: they defend those very few certainties holding together those incoherent structures of our personalities.

I believe that a synthesis between cautious communication and the need for decisive interventions must be found. It is similar to a physician who is obliged to communicate a diagnosis of a serious and distressing disease who, at the same time, wants to arouse the patient's internal strengths to positively deal with difficult therapy. Of course, here the disease is nothing but our consumerism and dissipative lifestyle, the waste, the excess, the financial speculation that reduced our world to a great casino, a disease that we still magnify in our current narratives as something good or even the only way to success and happiness! There are many similarities to substance or drug dependence.

It is fundamental that Schinaia's deep and thought-provoking reflections are not the solution we await but that unfortunately we do not have. Instead, they are an invitation to the entire community of scholars and physicians of the mind to work to find this solution. This must be a cultural solution to the ecological crisis that can face the deep emotional resistances that are hindrances to adequately using those advanced technological resources we have at our disposal.

References

Alighieri, D. (1314). *The Divine Comedy*. H.F. Cary (Trans.). Scotts Valley: CreateSpace Independent Publishing Platform, 2013.

Althusser, L. (1970). Ideology and ideological state apparatuses. B. Brewster (Trans.). In: J. Rivkin and M. Ryan (Eds.), *Literary Theory: An Anthology*. Second Edition (pp. 693–702). Oxford: Blackwell, 1998.

Ambrosiano, L. (2016). Introduzione. In: L. Ambrosiano and M. Sarno (Eds.), (pp. 11–21), op. cit.

Ambrosiano, L. (2017, January, 19). Fuori. Conference at the Centro Milanese di Psicoanalisi (Psychoanalytic Centre of Milan). Unpublished.

Ambrosiano, L. and Gaburri, E. (2013). *Pensare con Freud*. Milan: Cortina.

Ambrosiano, L. and Sarno, M. (Eds.). (2013). *Corruttori e Corrotti. Ipotesi Psicoanalitiche*. Milan-Udine: Mimesis.

American Psychiatric Association, DSM-5 Task Force. (2013). *Diagnostic and Statistical Manual of Mental Disorders: DSM-5™*. Fifth Edition. Washington, DC: American Psychiatric Publishing.

Amery, C. (1972). *Das Ende Vorsehung. Die Gnadenlosen Folgen des Christentums*. Hamburg: Rowholt Taschenbuch Verlag.

Amrine, M. (1946a, June, 23). The real problem is in the heart of men, *The New York Times Magazine*.

Amrine, M. (1946b, May, 25). Atomic education urged by Einstein, *The New York Times*.

Anders, G. (1980). *Die Antiquiertheit des Menschen 2. Über die Zerstörung des Lebens im Zeitalter der dritten industriellen Revolution. (The Outdatedness of Human Beings 2. On the Destruction of Life in the Era of the Third Industrial Revolution)*. Munich: C.H. Beck, 2002.

André, J. (2020). Malaise dans la Nature, malaise dans la culture. Prepublished paper for EPF Congress, Vienna, April 2–5, canceled because of COVID-19. http://epf-fep.eu/papers.

Anthes, E. (2020). *The Great Indoors. The Surprising Science of How Buildings Shape our Behaviour, Health and Happiness*. New York: Scientific American Books, Farrar, Straus & Giroux.

Arendt, H. (1968). *Men in Dark Times*. R. Winston and C. Winston (Trans.). Orlando: Harcourt Brace.

Arpaia, B. (2016). *Qualcosa, Là Fuori*. Parma: Guanda.

Arrhenius, S. (1896). On the influence of carbonic acid in the air upon the tempera-ture of the ground, *Philosophical Magazine and Journal of Science, 5, 41:* 237–276.

Arrhenius, S. (1906). Die Vorstellung vom Weltgebäude im Wandel der Zeiten: Das Werden der Welten, Neue Folge. Tr. all. L. Bamberger. Leipzig: Akademische Verlagsgesellschaft, 1908. En. tr.: Worlds in the Making: the Evolution of the Universe. H. Borns (Trans.). New York: Harper and Brothers, 1908.

Avallone, S. (2010). *Swimming to Elba.* A. Shugaar (Trans.). London: Viking, 2012.

Ballard, J.G. (1964). *The Burning World.* New York: Berkley Books.

Barthes, R. (1973). *The Pleasure of the Text.* R. Miller (Trans.). New York: Hill and Wang, 1975.

Bateson, G. (1972). *Steps to an Ecology of Mind: Collected Essays in Anthropology, Psychiatry, Evolution, and Epistemology.* Chicago, IL: Chicago University Press.

Baudrillard, J. (1978). Quand on enlève tout, il ne reste rien, *Traverses, 11:* 12–15.

Beigbeder, F. (2000). *£ 9.99.* A. Hunter (Trans.). London: Picador, 2002.

Bell, D. (2015). The death drive. Phenomenological perspectives in contemporary Kleinian theory, *International Journal of Psychoanalysis, 96, 2:* 411–423.

Bellamy, A. (2019). Trauma, fragmentation and narrative: Sándor Ferenczi's rele-vance for psychoanalytical perspectives on our response to climate change and environmental destruction, *International Journal of Applied Psychoanalytic Stud-ies: Climate Change and the Human Factor, 16, 2:* 100–108.

Benadusi, M. (2018). Oil in Sicily: Petrocapitalist imaginaries in the shadow of old smokestacks, *Economic Anthropology, 5, 1:* 45–58.

Benasayag, M. (2020, January, 23). Sono i nostri "Io" i nemici del Pianeta, *La Repubblica.*

Berger, C., & Roques, J.-L. (2016). *De la Crise Environnementale à l'Instabilité Identitaire.* Paris: Connaissances et Savoirs.

Bianchi, E. (2019, September, 28). Frate sole sorella luna perdonateci, *Robinson/La Repubblica.*

Binswanger, D. (2005). Il mondo fragile. Interview with Paul Virilio, *Internazionale, 12, 573:* 28–32.

Bion, W.R. (1961). *Experiences in Groups.* London: Tavistock.

Bion, W.R. (1962). A theory of thinking, *International Journal of Psycho-Analysis, 43:* 306–310.

Bion, W.R. (1978). *Wilfred Bion: Los Angeles Seminars and Supervision.* J. Aguayo and B. Malin (Eds.). London: Karnac, 2016.

Bion, W.R. (1990). *Brazilian Lectures. 1973 São Paulo. 1974 Rio de Janeiro/ São Paulo.* London: Karnac.

Bion, W.R. (1992). *Cogitations.* London: Karnac.

Boatti, G. (2012). *Sulle Strade dl Silenzio. Viaggio per Monasteri d'Italia e Spaesati Dintorni.* Rome-Bari: Laterza.

Boff, L. (2017). *Ética e Espiritualidade. Como Cuidar da Casa Comum.* São Paulo: Vozes.

Bollas, C. (2000). Architecture and the unconscious, *International Forum of Psycho-analysis, 9, 1:* 28–42.

Bollas, C. (2012). *China on the Mind.* London and New York: Routledge.

Bollas, C. (2017). *The Shadow of the Object.* Psychoanalysis of the Unthought Known. London and New York: Routledge.

Bollas, C. (2018). *Meaning and Melancholia. Life in the Age of Bewilderment.* London and New York: Routledge.

Brenman Pick, I. (2013). Discussion of the myth of apathy: Psychoanalytic explorations of environmental subjectivity. In: S. Weintrobe (Ed.). (pp. 134–137), op. cit.

Breton, A. (1942). Prolegomena to a third surrealist manifesto or not. In: R. Seaver and H. R. Lane (Trans.). *Manifestoes of Surrealism* (pp. 279–294). Ann Arbor: The University of Michigan Press, 1969.

Breuer, J. and Freud, J. (1893–1895). *Studies on Hysteria. S.E. 2*. London: Hogarth.

Breuer, J. and Freud, S. (1893). On the psychical mechanism of hysterical phenomena: Preliminary communication from studies on hysteria. *S.E. 2:* 1–17. London: Hogarth.

Buxton, R.T., McKenna, M.F., Mennit, D.J., Fristrup, K.M., Crooks, K., Angeloni, L., and Wittemeyer, G. (2017), Noise pollution is pervasive in U.S. protected areas. *Science, 356, 6337:* 531–533.

Calaprice, A., and Dyson, F. (Eds.), (2005). *The New Quotable Einstein*. Princeton, NJ: Princeton University Press.

Calvino, I. (1957). *The Baron in the Trees*. A. Colquhoun (Trans.). Boston, MA: Mariner Books, 1977.

Calvino, I. (1972). *Invisible Cities*. W. Weaver (Trans.). San Diego, CA: Harcourt, 1974.

Calvino, I. (1988). *Six Memos for The Next Millennium*. P. Creagh (Trans.). Harvard, MA: Harvard University Press.

Cameron, W.B. (1963). *Informal Sociology. A Casual Introduction to Sociological Thinking*. New York: Random House.

Camus, A. (1947). *The Plague*. S. Gilbert (Trans.). London: Penguin, 1960.

Cappiello, V. (2017). *Attraversare il Paesaggio*. Trento: List.

Capra, F. (1982). *The Turning Point: Science, Society, and the Rising Culture*. New York: Bantam Books.

Capra, F. and Mancuso, S. (2019). *Discorso sulle Erbe. Dalla Botanica di Leonardo alle Reti Vegetali*. Sansepolcro: Aboca.

Carloni, G. (1984). Tatto, contatto e tattica, *Rivista di Psicoanalisi, XXX, 2:* 191–205.

Caron, A. (2020). *La Revanche de la Nature*. Paris: Albin Michel.

Castoriadis, C. (2007). *La Montée de l'Insignifiance. Les Carrefours du Labyrinthe. IV.* Paris: Seuil.

Chianese, D. (2015). *Come le Pietre e gli Alberi. Psicoanalisi ed Estetica del Vivere.* Rome: Alpes Italia.

Chianese, D. (2018). Review of Prete, A. (2016). *Il Cielo Nascosto*, Turin: Bollati Boringhieri, *Rivista di Psicoanalisi, LXIV, 3:* 617–621.

Chiffoleau J. and Thomas Y. (2020). *L'Istituzione della Natura*. M. Spanò (It. Trans.). Macerata: Quodlibet.

Christin, R. (2014). *L'Usure du Monde. Critique de la Déraison Touristique*. Paris: L'Échappée.

Cianciullo, A. (2019). *Un Pianeta ad Aria Condizionata. Chi Paga il Conto del Global Warming?* Sansepolcro: Aboca.

Cirincione, E. (1991). *Ecologia e Psicoanalisi. Meccanismi Inconsci e Dinamiche Sociali della Crescente Distruttività Ambientale*. Padua: Muzzio.

Cohen, S. (2000). *States of Denial: Knowing about Atrocities and Suffering*. Cambridge, MA: Polity Press.

Coltart, N. (1993). *How to Survive as a Psychotherapist*. London: Sheldon Press.

Conrad, J. (1899). *Heart of Darkness*. New York: W. W. Norton & Company, 2016.

Corrado, M. (2012). *Il Sentiero dell'Architettura Porta nella Foresta*. Milan: FrancoAngeli.

Crutzen, P.J. and Stoermer, E.F. (2000). The "Anthropocene", Global Change Newsletter, *41*: 17–18.

Curtis, V. (2011). Why disgust matters, *Philosophical Transactions of the Royal Society. B. Biological Sciences, CCCLXVI, 1583*: 3478–3490.

Curtis, V. (2013). *Don't Look, Don't Touch: The Science behind Revulsion.* Oxford: Oxford University Press.

Danze, E.A. (2005). An architect's view of introspective space – The analytic vessel, *The Annual of Psychoanalysis, 33:* 109–124.

Darwin, C. (1859). *On the Origins of the Species.* Richmond, VA: Alma Classics, 2019.

Darwin, C. (1871). *The Descent of Man and Selection in Relation to Sex.* Princeton, NJ: Princeton University Press, 1981.

De Gregorio, C. (2013). *Io Vi Maledico.* Turin: Einaudi.

De Martino, E. (1977). *La Fine del Mondo. Contributo all'Analisi delle Apocalissi Culturali.* G. Charuty, D. Fabre and M. Massenzio (Eds.). Turin: Einaudi, 2019.

De Renzis, G. (2020). Personal communication in mailing list SPI.

De Tilla, M. and Militerni, L. (Eds.) (2019). *L'Inquinamento Indoor. Aspetti Architettonici, Bio-Giuridici e Medico-Scientifici dell'Abitare.* Milan: UTET.

DeLillo, D. (1997). *Underworld.* London: Picador.

Demailly, L. (2020). Malaise dans la civilisation et dans la psychanalyse: la question de la nature, *Le Coq Héron, 242*: 46–57.

Demetrio, D. (2005). *Filosofia del Camminare. Esercizi di Meditazione Mediterranea.* Milan: Cortina.

Derrida, J. (1976). Foreword. Fors. The English words of Nicolas Abraham and Maria Torok. In: Abraham, N. and Torok, M. *The Wolf Man's Magic Word. A Cryptonymy* (pp. xi–xvii). N. Rand (Trans.). Minneapolis: University of Minnesota Press.

Descola, Ph. (2005). *Beyond Nature and Culture.* J. Lloyd (Trans.). Chicago. IL: Chicago University Press, 2013.

Desveaux, J.-B. (2020). La crainte de l'effondrement climatique. Angoisses écologiques et incidences sur la psyché individuelle, *Le Coq Héron, 242*: 108–115.

Di Pietrantonio, D. (2020). *Borgo Sud.* Turin: Einaudi.

Diamond, J. (2005). *Collapse. How Societies Choose to Fail or Succeed.* London: Penguin Books.

Diamond, J. (2019). *Upheaval. Turning Points for Nations in Crisis.* Boston, MA: Little, Brown and Company.

Dodds, J. (2011). *Psychoanalysis and Ecology at the Edge of Chaos.* London and New York: Routledge.

Dorfles, G. (2008). *Horror Pleni. La (In)Civiltà del Rumore.* Rome: Castelvecchi.

Edwards, N. (2018). *Darkness. A Cultural History.* London: Reaktion Books.

Eliot, T.S. (1936). Burnt Norton. In: *Four Quartets* (pp. 13–22). Orlando: Harcourt, 1943.

Emery, N. (2007). *L'Architettura Difficile.* Milan: Marinotti.

Emery, N. (2011). *Distruzione e Progetto. L'Architettura Promessa.* Milan: Marinotti.

Engels, F. (1880). *Socialism: Utopian and Scientific.* E. Aveling (Trans.). London: Swan Sonnenschein, 1892.

Esposito, R. (2008). *Termini della Politica. Comunità, Immunità, Biopolitica. Volume 1.* Milan-Udine: Mimesis.

Esposito, R. (2016). *Da Fuori. Una Filosofia per l'Europa.* Turin: Einaudi.

Esposito, R. (2020, June, 20). Diritti di natura, *Robinson/La Repubblica.*

Fédida, P. *et al.* (2007). *Humain/Déshumain. La Parole de L'Oeuvre.* J. André (Ed.). Paris: PUF.

Ferenczi, S. (1924). *Thalassa. A Theory of Genitality.* H.A. Bunker (Trans.). London and New York: Routledge, 2018.

Ferenczi, S. (1928). The elasticity of psychoanalytic technique. In: *Final Contributions to the Problems and Methods of Psychoanalysis* (pp. 87–101). M. Balint (Ed.). E. Mosbacher *et al.* (Trans.). London and New York: Routledge, 1994.

Ferenczi, S. (1932). Confusion of the tongues between the adults and the child – The language of tenderness and of passion, *International Journal of Psycho-Analysis, 30:* 225–230, 1949.

Ferenczi, S. (1988). *The Clinical Diary of Sándor Ferenczi.* J. Dupont (Ed.). M. Balint and N. Z. Jackson (Trans.). Harvard, MA: Harvard University Press.

Ferruta, A. (2008). Crossing the bridge – Identità e cambiamento. In: *Identità e Cambiamento. Lo Spazio del Soggetto* (pp. 4–21). Proceedings of SPI (Italian Psychoanalytic Society). Rome: Gemmagraf.

Ferruta, A. (2020). Coronavirus: A Sphinx of modern times. Retrieved from https://www.cmp-spiweb.it/coronavirus-a-sphinx-of-modern-times/

Flegenheimer, F. (1986). Panel of Psychoanalytic Centre of Milan, October, cit. in Nissim Momigliano L., (1988, p. 609), op. cit.

Floridi, L. (2020). *Il Verde e il Blu. Idee Ingenue per Migliorare la Politica.* Milan: Cortina.

Foer, J.S. (2009). *Eating Animals.* London: Penguin.

Foer, J.S. (2019). *We Are the Weather. Saving the Planet Begins at Breakfast.* New York: Farrar, Straus & Giroux.

Fognini, M. (2020). À l'ère de catastrophes planétaires dépasser l' "egopsychanalyse" et l' "écologarchie", *Le Coq Héron, 242,* 3: 72–77.

Fornari, F. (1964). *Psicanalisi della Guerra Atomica.* Milan: Edizioni di Comunità.

Fornari, F. (1966). *The Psychoanalysis of War.* A. Pfeifer (Trans.). Bloomington: Indiana University Press, 1975.

Forrester, J.W. (1971). World dynamics, *Futures, 3, 2:* 162–169.

Foucault, M. (1966). The Thought of the Outside. In: *Essential Works of Foucault 1954–1984,* Vol. 2: *Aesthetics, Method, and Epistemology* (pp. 147–169). J.D. Faubion (Ed.). R. Hurley *et al.* (Trans.). New York: The New Press, 1998.

Foucault, M. (1984). *The History of Sexuality, Volume 3: The Care of the Self.* R. Hurley (Trans.). New York: Vintage Books, 1986.

Franzen, J. (2019). *What If We Stopped Pretending?* London: Fourth Estate, 2021.

Freud, A. (1936). *Ego and the Mechanisms of Defense.* C. Baines (Trans.). New York: International Universities Press, 1971.

Freud, S. (1900). The Interpretation of Dreams. *S.E. 4:* ix–627. London: Hogarth.

Freud, S. (1905). Three Essays on the Theory of Sexuality. *S.E. 7:* 123–246. London: Hogarth.

Freud, S. (1907). Delusions and Dreams in Jensen's "Gradiva". *S.E. 9:* 1–96. London: Hogarth.

Freud, S. (1911). Formulations on the Two Principles of Mental Functioning. *S.E. 12:* 213–226. London: Hogarth.

Freud, S. (1915). Thoughts for the Time on War and Death. *S.E. 14:* 289–300. London: Hogarth.

Freud, S. (1916a). Letter from Freud to Lou Andreas-Salomé, May 25. *The International Psycho-Analytical Library, 89*: 45

Freud, S. (1916b). On Transience. *S.E. 14:* 303–307. London: Hogarth.

Freud, S. (1917). Mourning and Melancholia. *S.E. 14: 237–258.* London: Hogarth.

Freud, S. (1918). From the History of an Infantile Neurosis. *S.E. 17:* 1–124. London: Hogarth.

Freud, S. (1919). The 'Uncanny'. *S.E. 17:* 217–256. London: Hogarth.

Freud, S. (1920). Beyond the Pleasure Principle. *S.E. 18:* 1–64. London: Hogarth.

Freud, S. (1923). The Ego and the Id. *S. E., 19:* 1–66. London: Hogart.

Freud, S. (1924). The Economic Problem of Masochism. *S.E. 19:* 155–170. London: Hogarth.

Freud, S. (1926). Inhibitions, Symptoms and Anxiety. *S.E. 20:* 75–176. London: Hogarth.

Freud, S. (1927a). The Future of an Illusion. *S.E. 21: 1–56.* London: Hogarth.

Freud, S. (1927b). Telegram to Anna Freud, April 24th. In: *Sigmund Freud-Anna Freud: Correspondence 1904–1938.* I. Meyer-Palmed (Ed.). N. Somers (Trans.). Cambridge, MA: Polity Press.

Freud, S. (1930). Civilization and Its Discontents. *S.E. 21:* 59.145. London: Hogarth.

Freud, S. (1933). Sándor Ferenczi. *S.E. 22:* 227–232. London: Hogarth.

Freud, S. (1937). Constructions in Analysis. *S.E. 23:* 255–270. London: Hogarth.

Freud, E.L. (Ed.). *Letters of Sigmund Freud.* T. and J. Stern (Trans.). New York: Dover Publications, 1992.

Gadda, C.E. (1959). La nostra casa si trasforma: e l'inquilino la deve subire. In: D. Isella, C. Martignoni and L. Orlando (Eds.). *Saggi, Giornali, Favole. Volume I* (pp. 373–397). Milan: Garzanti, 1991.

Galimberti, U. (2019, January, 26). L'etica per la natura, *D La Repubblica*.

Gallione, A. (2019, September, 13). Comincia in città il rinascimento dei nostri boschi. Interview with Stefano Boeri, *La Repubblica*.

Garrett, J.K., Donald, P.F., and Gaston, K.J. (2020). Skyglow extends into the world's key biodiversity areas, *Animal Conservation, 23, 2:* 153–159.

Gatti, C. (2019, December, 20). Noi artisti siamo i giardinieri del pianeta. Interview to Michelangelo Pistoletto, *La Repubblica*.

Ghosh, A. (2016). *The Great Derangement. Climate Change and the Unthinkable.* Chicago, IL: University of Chicago Press.

Giblett, R. (2019). *Psychoanalytic Ecology. The Talking Cure for Environmental Illness and Health.* London and New York: Routledge.

Gnoli, A. and Volpi, F. (2003). In viaggio con Freud. In: C. Togel (Ed.). *Il Nostro Cuore Volge al Sud. Lettere di Viaggio, Soprattutto dall'Italia* (pp. 5–10). Milan: Bompiani, 2003.

Goldmann, I. (2019). Le basi del concetto di sostenibilità di uno spazio. In: M. De Tilla and L. Militerni (Eds.) (2018). *L'Inquinamento Indoor. Aspetti Architettonici, Bio-Giuridici e Medico-Scientifici dell'Abitare* (pp. 3–35). Milan: UTET.

Goldmann, I., Redaelli, E., and Cerveglieri, G. (2019). Dove si generano in architettura le problematiche conseguenti all'inquinamento *indoor* e come si risolvono con la bioarchitettura. In: M. De Tilla and L. Militerni (Eds.), (pp. 78–134), op. cit.

Granieri, A. (2016). La comunità contaminata di Casale Monferrato: Aspetti corruttivi della *governance* e sopravvivenza psichica. In: L. Ambrosiano and M. Sarno (Eds.). (pp. 107–126), op. cit.

Greenpeace. (2016). La plastica nel piatto, Dal pesce ai frutti di mare, https://www.greenpeace.org/italy/Global/italy/report/.../mare/la plastica-nel-piatto.pdf

Groddeck, G. (1923). *The Book of the It. Psychoanalytic Letters to a Friend.* New York: Nervous and Mental Disease Publishing Company, 1928.

Grotstein, J.S. (2007). *A Beam of Intense Darkness.* Wilfred Bion's Legacy to Psychoanalysis. London and New York: Routledge.

Halfwerk, W., Bot, S., Buikx, J., van der Velde, M., Komdeur, J., ten Cate, C., and Slabbekoorn, H. (2011). Low-frequency songs lose their potency in noisy urban conditions, *PNAS (Proceedings of the National Academy of Sciences of the USA),* August 30, *108, 35:* 14549–14554.

Hamilton, C. (2010). *Requiem for a Species. Why We Resist the Truth about Climate Change.* London: Earthscan.

Hamilton, C. (2013). What history can teach us about climate change denial. In: S. Weintrobe (Ed.), (pp. 16–32), op. cit.

Harari, Y.N. (2011). *Sapiens. A Brief History of Humankind.* New York: Vintage, 2014.

Haseley, D. (2019). Climate change: Clinical considerations, *International Journal of Applied Psychoanalytic Studies: Climate Change and the Human Factor, 16, 2:* 109–115.

Hegel, G.W.F. (1812–1816). *Science of Logic.* G. Di Giovanni (Trans.). Cambridge: Cambridge University Press, 2010.

Heller, Á. (1974). *The Theory of Need in Marx.* London: Allison and Busby, 1976.

Hoggett, P. (2013). Climate change in a perverse culture. In: S Weintrobe (Ed.), (pp. 56–71), op. cit.

Irigaray, L. (2011). Perhaps cultivating touch can still save us, *SubStance, 126, 40, 3:* 130–140.

Jamieson, D., and Mancuso, S. (2017, April, 16). La scienza e l'effetto Trump, *La Repubblica.*

Jemisin, N.K. (2015). *The Fifth Season. The Broken Earth #1.* London: Orbit.

Jonas, H. (1979). The Imperative of Responsibility. In: *Search of an Ethics for the Technological Age.* H. Jonas and D. Herr (Trans.). Chicago, IL: University of Chicago Press.

Jones, E. (1953). *The Life and Work of Sigmund Freud.* L. Trilling and S. Marcus (Eds.). London: Penguin Books.

Jucovy, M.E. (1992). Psychoanalytical contributions to Holocaust studies, *International Journal of Psychoanalysis, 73:* 267–291.

Jung, C.G. (1961). The tour. In: C.G. Jung and A. Jaffé, (pp. 225–228), op. cit.

Jung, C.G. (1962). *Memories, Dreams, Reflections.* A. Jaffé (Ed.). R. Winston and C. Winston (Trans.). New York: Pantheon Books.

Kaës, R. (1993). Le sujet de l'héritage. In: Kaës, R., Faimberg, H., Enriquez, M. and Baranes, J.-J., *Transmission de la Vie Psychique entre Générations* (p. 1–16). Paris: Dunod.

Kaës, R. (2012). *Le Malêtre.* Paris: Dunod.

Kaës, R. (2013, April 13). Malessere sociale e malessere individuale: alleati o nemici? In: Seminar AFPP CSMH – AMHPPIA SIPP SPI "Malessere sociale e malessere individuale: alleati o nemici?", Centro Psicoanalitico Firenze (Psychoanalytic Center of Florence, IT). https://www.spi-firenze.it/category/eventi/archivio-relazioni

Kakar, S. (1997). *Culture and Psyche. Selected Essays.* Oxford: Oxford University Press.

Keene, J. (2013). Unconscious obstacles to caring for the planet. Facing up to human Nature. In: S. Weintrobe (Ed.), (pp. 144–159), op. cit.

Kestenberg, J. (1989). Transposition revised: Clinical, therapeutic and developmental considerations. In: P. Marcus and A. Rosenberg (Eds.). *Healing Their Wounds. Psychotherapy with Holocaust Survivors and their Families* (pp. 67–82). New York: Praeger.

Khan, M.M.R. (1983). *Hidden Selves. Between Theory and Practice in Psychoanalysis.* London: Routledge.

Klein, M. (1935). A contribution to the psychogenesis of manic-depressive states. In: *Love, Guilt and Reparation and Other Works 1921–1945* (pp. 262–289). New York: The Free Press, 1975.

Klein, M. (1946). Notes on some schizoid mechanisms. In: *Envy and Gratitude and Other Works 1946–1963* (pp. 1–24). London: Vintage.

Kohut, H. (1981). On the continuity of the self and cultural selfobjects. In: C.B. Strozier (Ed.). *Self Psychology and the Humanities. Reflections on a New Psychoanalytic Approach* (pp. 232–243). New York & London: Norton & Company, 1985.

Lacan, J. (1959–1960). *The Seminar of Jacques Lacan: The Ethics of Psychoanalysis (Book VII).* D. Porter (Trans.). New York: Norton, 1992.

Lacan, J. (1964). *The Four Fundamental Concepts of Psychoanalysis,* A. Sheridan (Trans.). London: Penguin, 1979.

Lagomarsini, S. (2017). *Coltivare e Custodire. Per una Ecologia senza Miti.* Firenze: Libreria Editrice Fiorentina.

Laing, R.D. (1967). *The Politics of Experience and the Bird of Paradise.* London: Penguin Books.

Landrigan, P.J., *et al.* (2017). The *Lancet* Commission on Pollution and Health, *Lancet* (published *online*, October 19).

Lanternari, V. (2003). *Ecoantropologia. Dall'Ingerenza Ecologica alla Svolta Etico-Culturale.* Bari: Dedalo.

Latouche, S. (2007). *Farewell to Growth.* D. Macey (Trans.). Cambridge, MA: Polity Press, 2009.

Latour, B. (2015). *Facing Gaia: Eight Lectures on the New Climatic Regime.* C. Porter (Trans.). Cambridge, MA: Polity, 2017.

Lauret, M. (2020). Que peut nous enseigner la crise chinoise du Covid-19? Retrieved from https://mailchi.mp/f677ece6ec42/des-nouvelles-de-chine?e=efbad4f646

Le Roy Ladurie, E. (1967). *Times of Feast, Times of Famine. A History of Climate since the Year 1000.* B. Bray (Trans.). New York: Farrar, Straus & Giroux, 2011.

Leogrande, A. (2018). *Dalle Macerie. Cronache sul Fronte Meridionale.* Milan: Feltrinelli.

Leopardi, G. (1817–1832). *Zibaldone: The Notebook of Leopardi.* M. Caesar and F. D'Intino (Eds.). New York: Farrar, Straus & Giroux, 2013.

Leopardi, G. (1824). Dialogue of Nature and an Icelander. In: *The Moral Essays (Operette Morali).* P. Creagh (Trans.). New York: Columbia University Press, 1983.

Lertzman, R.A. (2013). The myth of apathy. Psychoanalytic explorations of environmental subjectivity. In S. Weintrobe (Ed.) (pp. 115–133), op. cit.

Lertzman, R.A. (2015). *Environmental Melancholia: Psychoanalytic Dimensions of Engagement.* London and New York: Routledge.

Levi, P. (1947). *If This Is a Man.* S. Woolf (Trans.). London: The Orion Press, 1959.

Liberman, D. (1970–1972). *Lingüística, Interacción Comunicativa y Proceso Psico-analítico. Volumes I-III.* Buenos Aires: Galerna.

Lilla, M. (2016). *The Shipwrecked Mind. On Political Reaction.* New York: New York Review Books.

Lingiardi, V. (2017). *Mindscapes. Psiche nel Paesaggio.* Milan: Cortina.

Lombardozzi, A. (2006). Gaia. Riflessioni a proposito del libro *Ecoantropologia* di Vittorio Lanternari. In: *Figure del Dialogo tra Antropologia e Psicoanalisi* (pp. 152–164). Rome: Borla.

Lombardozzi, A. (2020). Cambiamenti climatici e crisi ambientale. Pensieri psico-analitici su un'ecologia antropologica, *Rivista di Psicoanalisi, LXVI, 3*: 669–685.

Lynch, K. (1990). *Wasting Away. An Exploration of Waste: What It Is, How It Happens, Why We Fear It, How To Do It Well.* M. Southworth (Ed.). New York: Random House.

Lynch, K. and Hack, G. (1962). *Site Planning.* Cambridge, MA: MIT Press.

Magnason, A.S. (2019). *On Tine and Water.* L. Smith (Trans.). London: Profile Books, 2020.

Magnenat, L. (2019a). Introduction. In: L. Magnenat (Ed.). *La Crise Environnemen-tale sur le Divan* (pp. 1–8). Paris: In Press.

Magnenat, L. (2019b). Les processus inconscients en jeu dans la crise environne-mentale: l'article d'un pionnier de la psychanalyse intéressée à l'écologie, Harold Searles. In: L. Magnenat (Ed.), (pp. 26–28), op. cit.

Magnenat, L. (2019c). Le propre de l'homme à l'âge de l'Anthropocène: *Homo Sapiens Demens.* In L. Magnenat (Ed.), (pp. 145–248), op. cit.

Malidelis, D. (2019). La psicoanalisi di fronte alla crisi ecologica. Interview to Cosimo Schinaia. Retrieved from http://www.psychoanalysis.gr/index.php/dialogue?id=141.

Mancuso, S. (2019). *La Nazione delle Piante.* Bari-Rome: Laterza.

Mancuso, S. (2020, July, 1). Curiamo le metropoli come fossero piante, *La Repubblica.*

Manguel, A. (2007). *The City of Words (CBC Massy Lecture).* Toronto: House of Anansi.

Mann, T. (1936). Freud and the future. In: *Death in Venice, Tonio Kroeger and Other Writings* (pp. 279–296). H.T. Lowe-Porter (Trans.). F. Lubich (Ed.). New York: Continuum.

Mappa, S. (2020). Le morcellement du monde. Environnement et psychanalyse, *Le Coq Héron, 242:* 58–67.

Marcuse, H. (1955). *Eros and Civilization. A Philosophical Inquiry into Freud.* Boston, MA: Beacon Press.

Marshall, G. (2005). Sleepwalking into disaster. Are we in a state of denial about climate change? Retrieved from http://coinet.org.uk/information/perspectives/marshal

Marx, K. (1841). *The Difference between the Democritean and Epicurean Philosophy of Nature.* B. Baggins (Ed. and Trans.). Retrieved from www.marxist.org

Marx, K. (1844). *Economic and Philosophic Manuscripts of 1844.* M. Milligan (Trans.). New York: Dover, 2007.

Marx, K. (1867). *Capital. Volume I.* B. Fowkes (Trans.). London: Penguin, 1990.

Mathieu, N. (2018). *And Their Children after Them.* W. Rodarmor (Trans.). New York: Other Press, 2020.

Matot, J.-P. (2020). *Le Soi-Disséminé. Une Perspective Écosystémique et Métapsychologique*. Paris: L'Harmattan.

Mauri, P. (2007). *Buio*. Turin: Einaudi.

McGuire, W. and Hull, R.F.C. (1977). *C.G. Jung Speaking. Interviews and Encounters*. Princeton, NJ: Princeton University Press.

Meadows, D.H., Meadows, Dennis L., Randers, J., and Behrens III, W.W. (1972). *The Limits to Growth*. New York: Universe Books.

Meltzer, D. (1967). *The Psychoanalytical Process*. London: Heinemann Medical Books.

Meltzer, D. (1986). *Studies of Extended Metapsychology. Clinical Applications of Bion's Ideas*. London: Harris Meltzer Trust; revised edition, 2018.

Meotti, F. (1992). Review of Cirincione, E. (1991). *Ecologia e Psicoanalisi*, Padua: Muzzio, *Rivista di Psicoanalisi, XXXVIII, 2:* 546–548.

Mercalli, L. (2016). *Il Mio Orto tra Cielo e Terra. Appunti di Meteorologia e Ecologia Agraria per Salvare Clima e Cavoli*. San Sepolcro: Aboca.

Mercalli, L. (2018). *Non c'è Più Tempo. Come Reagire agli Allarmi Ambientali*. Turin: Einaudi.

Merlo, F. (2018, August, 10). Tornate indietro. Pronti a organizzare un Periferia Pride. Interview with Renzo Piano, *La Repubblica*.

Miller, S.B. (1986). Disgust: Conceptualization, development and dynamics, *International Review of Psychoanalysis, 13:* 295–307.

Miller, S.B. (1993). Disgust reactions. Their determinants and manifestations in treatment, *Contemporary Psychoanalysis, 29:* 711–734.

Mirzoeff, N. (2015). *How to See the World*. London: Penguin.

Mistura, S. (2001). Introduzione. In: S. Mistura (Ed.) *Figure del Feticismo* (pp. VII–XXVI). Turin: Einaudi.

Monterosa, L. (2013). Lo spazio sonoro nella stanza di analisi, *Rivista di Psicoanalisi, LIX, 3:* 573–590.

Monti, M. and Redi, C.A. (Eds.). (2019). *Con-dividuo. Cellule e Genomi XVII Corso: I Corsi dell'Open Lab*. Pavia: Ibis.

Moore, C. and Phillips, C. (2011). *Plastic Ocean: How a Sea Captain's Chance Discovery Launched a Determined Quest to Save the Oceans*. New York: Avery.

Moresco, A. (2018). *Il Grido*. Milan: SEM.

Morin, E. (2016). *Écologiser l'Homme. La Nature du Futur et le Futur de la Nature*. Paris: Lemieux.

Morton, T. (2007). *Ecology without Nature: Rethinking Environmental Aesthetics*. Harvard, MA: Harvard University Press.

Nancy, J.-L. (2014). After tragedy. In: L. Cull Ó Maoilearca and A. Lagaay (Eds.). *Encounters in Performance Philosophy* (pp. 279–289). London: Palgrave Macmillan.

Neri, M. (2020, March, 17). Amare e sperare di questi tempi. Interview with Jenny Offill, *La Repubblica*.

Nicholsen, S.W. (2002). *The Love of Nature and the End of the World: The Unspoken Dimensions of Environmental Concern*. Cambridge, MA: MIT Press.

Niola, M. (2020, January, 4). Non si tratta solo di carne si o no. Etica, coscienza, ambiente, rapporti con le altre specie. È arrivato il momento di confrontarsi senza fanatismo e sarcasmo, *La Repubblica*.

Nissim Momigliano, L. (1988). Il *setting*: tema con variazioni, *Rivista di Psicoanalisi, XXXIV, 4:* 604–683.

Odum, E.P. (1983). *Basic Ecology*. San Diego, CA: Harcourt Brace.

Offil, J. (2020). *Weather. A Novel*. New York: Alfred A. Knopf.

Pallasmaa, J.U. (2004). Introduzione. In: Martellotti, D. *Architettura dei Sensi* (pp. 13–16). Rome: Mancosu.

Pasolini, P.P. (1959). *The Long Road of Sand*. S. Sartarelli (Trans.). Rome: Contrasto, 2015.

Pasolini, P.P. (1975). Disappearance of the fireflies. Retrieved from https://www.diagonalthoughts.com/?p=2107

Pavese, C. (1950). *The Moon and the Bonfires*. R.W. Flint (Trans.). New York: New York Review Books, 2002.

Pera, P. (2016). *Al Giardino Ancora non l'ho Detto*. Milan: Ponte alle Grazie.

Pichon-Rivière, E. (1971). *El Proceso Grupal. Del Psicoanálisis a la Psicología Social*. Buenos Aires: Nueva Visión.

Plato (385-370 BC). *The Symposium*. C. Gill (Ed. and Trans.). London: Penguin Books, 2003.

Plummer, H. (2016). *The Experience of Architecture*. London: Thames Hudson.

Polla-Mattiot, N. (2017). Pieno e vuoto. In: M. Francesconi and D. Scotto di Fasano (Eds.). *Aree di Confine. Cosa, Corpo, Parole tra Filosofia e Psicoanalisi* (pp. 159–167). Milan-Udine: Mimesis.

Pontalis, J.-B. (1986). *Love of Beginnings*. J. Greene (Trans.). London: Free Association Books, 1993.

Pope Francis. (2015). *Laudato Si'. On Care for Our Common Home*. Vatican City: Libreria Editrice Vaticana.

Popper, K.R. (1945). *The Open Society and Its Enemies*. London: Routledge.

Porter, S.D., Reay, D.S., Bomberg, E., and Higgins, P. (2018). Avoidable food Losses and Associated Production-Phase Greenhouse Gas Emissions Arising from Application of Cosmetic Standards to Fresh Fruit and Vegetables in Europe and the UK, *Journal of Cleaner Production, 20, 10:* 869–878.

Powers, R. (2018). *The Overstory*. New York: W.W. Norton & Company.

Press, J. (2019). Psychanalyse et crise environnementale. In: L. Magnenat (Ed.) (pp. 261–270), op. cit.

Preta, L. (2018). Review of Lingiardi, V. (2017). *Mindscapes. Psiche nel Paesaggio,* Milan: Cortina, *Rivista di Psicoanalisi, LXIV, 1:* 197–201.

Preta, L. (2019a). *The Brutality of Things. Psychic Transformations of Reality*. Milan-Udine: Mimesis-International.

Preta, L. (2019b). Breve storia di Geografie della psicoanalisi, *Psiche, 2:* 571–583.

Prete, A. (2016). *Il Cielo Nascosto. Grammatica dell'Interiorità*. Turin: Bollati Boringhieri.

Puget, J. and Wender, L. (1982). Analista y paciente en mundos superpuestos, *Psicoanálisis, 4, 3:* 503–536.

Quammen, D. (2012). *Spillover. Animal Infections and the Next Human Pandemic*. New York: W.W. Norton Company.

Quammen, D. (2018). *The Tangled Tree. A Radical New History of Life*. New York: Simon & Schuster.

Quinodoz, D. (2002). *Words That Touch: A Psychoanalyst Learns to Speak*. Ph. Slotkin (Trans.). London: Karnac, 2003.

Randall, R. (2005). A new climate for psychotherapy? *Psychotherapy and Politics International, 3:* 165–179.

Randall, R. (2009). Loss and climate change: The cost of the parallel narratives, *Ecopsychology, 3:* 165–179.

Ravignant, P. (1960). *The Cities of the Bald.* London: Barrie & Rockliff.

Rea, E. (2002). *La Dismissione.* Milan: Rizzoli.

Rhys, J. (1934). *Voyage in the Dark.* London: Penguin, 2000.

Ricci, G. (1995). *Le Città di Freud. Itinerari, Emblemi, Orizzonti di un Viaggiatore.* Milan: Jaca Book.

Rich, N. (2019). *Losing Earth. A Recent History.* New York: Farrar, Straus & Giroux.

Rifkin, J. and Howard, T. (1980). *Entropy.* New York: Viking Press.

Rigotti, F. (2020). *Buio.* Bologna: Il Mulino.

Rimbaud, A. (1886). *Illuminations and Other Prose Poems.* L. Varèse (Trans.). New York: New Directions, 1957.

Romeo, S. (2018). Introduzione. In: Leogrande, A. *Dalle Macerie. Cronache sul Fronte Meridionale* (pp. 15–22). Milan: Feltrinelli.

Roszak, T. (2009). A Psyche as big as the Earth. In: L. Buzzell and C. Chalquist (Eds.) (2009). *Ecotherapy: Healing with Nature in Mind* (pp. 30–36). San Francisco, CA: Sierra Club Books.

Russo, M. (2016). Uscire dalla psicosi urbana: per una nuova idea di comunità. In: A. D'Angiò, M. Guelfo, and D. Mazzoleni (Eds.). *La Città Psicotica* (pp. 59–66). Naples: Guida.

Rust, M.-J. (2008). Climate on the couch: Unconscious processes in relation to our environmental crisis, *Psychotherapy and Politics International, 6, 3:* 157–170.

Rustin, M. (2013). How is climate change an issue for psychoanalysis? In: S. Weintrobe, S. (Ed.), (pp. 170–185), op. cit.

Rykwert, J. (1963). *The Idea of a Town. The Anthropology of Urban Form in Rome, Italy and the Ancient World.* Cambridge, MA: MIT Press, 1988.

Rykwert, J. (2000). *The Seduction of Place. The History and Future of Cities.* London: Vintage Books.

Sacks, J. (2020). *Morality: Restoring the Common Good in Divided Times.* London: Basic Books.

Salomé, L.A. (1958). *The Freud Journal.* S. A. Leavy (Trans.). London: Quartet Books, 1987.

Saramago, J. (1995). *Blindness.* G. Pontiero (Trans.). San Diego, CA: Harcourt Publishing.

Sarno, M. (2016). 'Tempi che strapiombano': Note di psicoanalisi allargata 'sopra lo stato presente dei costumi degli italiani'. Illegalità, corruzione, criminalità. In: L. Ambrosiano e M. Sarno (Eds.). (pp. 25–43), op. cit.

Saviano, R. (2006). *Gomorrah. Italy's Other Mafia.* V. Jewiss (Trans.). New York: Farrar, Straus & Giroux.

Scaffai, N. (2017). *Letteratura e Ecologia. Forme e Temi di una Relazione Narrativa.* Rome: Carocci.

Scanlan, J. (2005). *On Garbage.* London: Reaktion Books.

Schiavone, A. (2020). *Progresso.* Bologna: Il Mulino.

Schinaia, C. (2001). *On Paedophilia.* A. Sansone (Trans.). London: Karnac, 2010. Republished London and New York: Routledge, 2018.

Schinaia, C. (2014). *Psychoanalysis and Architecture. The Inside and the Outside.* G. Lo Dico (Trans.). London: Karnac, 2016. Republished London and New York: Routledge, 2018.

Schinaia, C. (2016). *Interno Esterno. Sguardi Psicoanalitici su Architettura e Urbanistica.* Rome: Alpes Italia.

Schinaia, C. (2018). L'inconscient coquin d'un "enfant perdu". L'aventure inquiétante de Freud à Gênes, *Revue Française de Psychanalyse, LXXXII, 5:* 1495–1500.

Schinaia, C. (2019a). Respect for the environment. Psychoanalytic reflections on the ecological crisis, *International Journal of Psychoanalysis, 100, 2:* 272–286.

Schinaia, C. (2019b). Facing up to the risks of climate change, IPA Website. https://www.ipa.world/en/News/News_articles_reviews/Officers_blog.aspx.

Searles, H.F. (1960). *The Nonhuman Environment: In Normal Development and Schizophrenia.* Madison, WI: International Universities Press.

Searles, H.F. (1972). Unconscious processes in relation to the environmental crisis, *Psychoanalytic Review, 59, 3:* 361–374.

Segal, H. (1987). Silence is the real crime, *International Review of Psychoanalysis, 14:* 3–12.

Sennett, R. (2018). *Building and Dwelling. Ethics for the City.* London: Allen Lane.

Settis, S. (2013). *Il Paesaggio come Bene Comune.* Naples: La Scuola di Pitagora.

Simmel, G. (1903). The metropolis of modern life. In: D. Levine (Ed.). *Simmel. On Individuality and Social Forms* (pp. 324–339). Chicago, IL: Chicago University Press, 1971.

Smith, V. (2018). *Clean, A History of Personal Hygiene and Purity.* Oxford: Oxford University Press.

Spitz, R.A. (1965). *The First Year of Life. A Psychoanalytic Study of Normal and Deviant Development of Object Relations.* New York: International Universities Press.

Steiner, J. (2018). Time and the Garden of Eden illusion, *International Journal of Psychoanalysis, 99, 6:* 1274–1287.

Steiner, R. (1989). It's a new kind of diaspora…, *International Review of Psychoanalysis, 16:* 35–78.

Stoll-Kleemann, S., O'Riordan, T., and Jaeger, C.C. (2001). The psychology of denial concerning climate mitigation measures: Evidence from Swiss focus group, *Global Environmental Change, 11:* 107–117.

Storr, A. (1972). *Human Destructiveness. The Roots of Genocide and Human Cruelty.* London and New York: Routledge, 2014.

Stuart-Smith, S. (2020). *The Well Gardened Mind: Rediscover Nature in the Modern World.* Glasgow: William Collins.

Tanizaki, J. (1933). *In Praise of Shadows.* E.G. Seidensticker and T.J. Harper (Trans.). Sedgwick: Leete's Island Books, 1977.

Tedesco, M. (with the coll. of Flores D'Arcais, A.) (2019). *Ghiaccio. Viaggio nel Continente che Scompare.* Milan: Il Saggiatore.

Thoreau, H.D. (1854). *Walden; or, Life in the Woods.* New York: Dover, 1995.

Thunberg, G. (2019). *No One Is Too Small to Make a Difference.* London: Penguin.

Thunberg, G., Thunberg, S., Ernman, M. and Ernman, B. (2020). *Our House Is on Fire: Scenes of a Family and a Planet in Crisis.* P. Norlen and S. Vogel (Trans.). London: Penguin.

Tögel, Ch. (Ed.), with the coll. of Molnar M. (2002). *Unser Herz zeigt nach dem Süden: Reisebriefe 1895–1923* [Our Heart Points to the South: Travel Letters 1895–1923]. Sigmund Freud. Berlin: Aufbau-Verlag, 2002. *Sigmund Freud. Il nostro Cuore Volge al Sud. Lettere di Viaggio, Soprattutto dall'Italia (1895–1923).* G. Rovagnati (It. Trans.). Milan: Bompiani, 2003.

Trosman, H. and Simmons, R.D. (1973). The Freud library, *Journal of American Psychoanalytic Association, 21*, 3: 646–687.

Van Aken, M. (2020). *Campati per Aria*. Milan: Eleuthera.

Vassallo Torrigiani, M.G. (2014, December). Psicoanalisi e 'crisi ecologica'. Retrieved from https://www.spiweb.it›dossier›per-una-nuova-ecologia-dicembre-2014

Venturi Ferrioli, M. (2019). *Oltre il Giardino. Filosofia del Paesaggio*. Turin: Einaudi.

Videtti, G. (2019, July, 19). Tutta un'altra musica. Interview with Theodor Currentzis, *Il Venerdì di Repubblica*.

Viola, A. (2020). *Flower Power. Le Piante e i Loro Diritti*. Turin: Einaudi.

Virgil (29 BC–19 BC). *The Aeneid*. R. Fitzgerald (Trans.). London: Vintage.

Voltaire. (1759). *Candide*. S.G. Corcos (Trans.). New York: Dover, 1991.

Weber, M. (1919). Politics as a vocation. In: T. and D. Waters (Eds. and Trans.). *Weber's Rationalism and Modern Society. New Translations on Politics, Bureaucracy, and Social Stratification* (pp. 129–178). New York: Palgrave Macmillan.

Weintrobe, S. (2013a). Introduction. In: S. Weintrobe (Ed.), (pp. 1–15), op. cit.

Weintrobe, S. (2013b). The difficult problem of anxiety in thinking about climate change. In: S. Weintrobe (Ed.), (pp. 33–47), op. cit.

Weintrobe, S. (2013c). On the Love of Nature and on Human Nature. Restoring Split Internal Landscapes. In: S. Weintrobe (Ed.), (pp. 199–213), op. cit.

Weintrobe, S. (Ed.). (2013d). *Engaging with the Climate Change: Psychoanalysis and Interdisciplinary Perspective*. London and New York: Routledge.

Weintrobe, S. (2019). On Climate Change Denial, IPA website. Retrieved from http://www.sallyweintrobe.com/about-sally/

Winnicott, D.W. (1960). The theory of the parent-infant relationship, *International Journal of Psychoanalysis, 41:* 585–595.

Winnicott, D.W. (1965). *The Maturational Processes and the Facilitating Environment: Studies in the Theory of Emotional Development*. New York: International Universities Press.

Winnicott, D.W. (1969). Berlin walls. In: C. Winnicott, R. Shepherd, and M. Davis. *Home Is Where We Start From: Essays by a Psychoanalyst* (pp. 221–227). London: Penguin, 1986.

Winnicott, D.W. (1974). Fear of breakdown, *International Review of Psycho-Analysis, 1(1–2):* 103–107.

Zagaria, C. (2013). *Veleno. La Battaglia di una Giovane Donna nella Città Ostaggio dell'Ilva*. Milan: Sperling & Kupfer.

Zagrebelsky, G. (2017). *Diritti per Forza*. Turin: Einaudi.

Zanzotto, A. (2013). *Luoghi e Paesaggi*. Milan: Bompiani.

Zeniter, A. (2017). *The Art of Losing*. F. Wynne (Trans.). New York: Farrar, Straus and Giroux, 2021.

Žižek, S. (1992). *Looking Awry. An Introduction to Lacan Trough Popular Culture*. Cambridge, MA: MIT Press.

Žižek, S. (2007). Censorship today: Violence or ecology as a new opium for the masses. Retrieved from http://www.lacan.com/zizecology1.htm

Zoja, L. (2017). *Nella Mente di un Terrorista. Conversazione con Omar Bellicini*. Turin: Einaudi.

Index

Note: Page numbers followed by "n" denote endnotes.

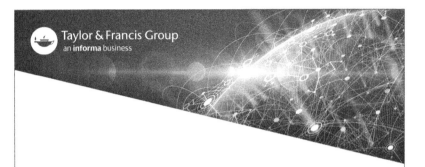